The Laurel and Hardy Legacy

Sitcom Stars Talk Stan and Ollie

Barry Brophy

DARK RIVER

Published in 2016 by Dark River, an imprint of Bennion Kearny Limited.

Copyright © Dark River

ISBN: 978-1-911121-17-6

All Rights Reserved. No part of this publication may be reproduced, stored in a retrieval system, or transmitted in any form or by any means, electronic, mechanical, photocopying, recording or otherwise, without the prior permission of the publisher.

This book is sold subject to the condition that it shall not, by way of trade or otherwise, be lent, re-sold, hired out or otherwise circulated without the publisher's prior consent in any form of binding or cover other than that it which it is published and without a similar condition including this condition being imposed on the subsequent purchaser.

Dark River has endeavoured to provide trademark information about all the companies and products mentioned in this book by the appropriate use of capitals. However, Dark River cannot guarantee the accuracy of this information.

Published by Dark River, an imprint of Bennion Kearny Limited
6 Woodside
Churnet View Road
Oakamoor
ST10 3AE

This book is dedicated to my brother and friends who grew up with me and with Laurel and Hardy.

About the Author

Barry Brophy is a writer and a lecturer in communications at University College Dublin. He is married with two young children who, having only seen Laurel and Hardy a handful of times, christened them, 'Fall Down.'

Acknowledgements

I would like to thank all of the contributors who gave up their valuable time to talk to me when they must have had a great many more pressing things to do. I would also like to thank all the agents, PA's, and publicists who dealt with my correspondence and occasionally put in a good word on my behalf.

Laurel and Hardy made their greatest films between 1926 and 1940. Over seven decades later, many of the top names in comedy still cite them as both key influences and favourites. This book is based on a set of interviews with some of the biggest names in television comedy who talk about the greatest double act of all time and parallels with their own work.

Ray Galton and Alan Simpson were interviewed together and, for that reason, I didn't distinguish who said what. The only other quotations, taken from rare interviews given in the late 1940s and 1950s, are from Stan Laurel and Oliver Hardy themselves.

Table of Contents

1. Characters	1
2. Stan	13
3. Oliver Norvell Hardy	23
4. Space	31
5. Story	41
6. Actions & Reactions	59
7. Supporting Roles	75
8. Rise & Fall	81
9. Endurance	89
10. Last Laugh	97
Filmography	101
Bibliography	106
Epilogue	107

Contributors

Ardal O'Hanlon is most famous for playing Father Dougal in *Father Ted*. He has starred in several other TV sitcoms, written fiction, and performed stand-up.

Stephen Merchant is a writer and comedy actor best known for his work on *The Office* and *Extras*. He has co-written and appeared in several other films and TV shows.

Bruce Forsyth's legendary stage and television career spans six decades. He most recently hosted hit the BBC series *Strictly Come Dancing*.

Tony Robinson's most famous comic role was as Baldrick in *Blackadder*. He has a prolific career hosting history programmes and writing children's books.

Richard Wilson's most famous role was as Victor Meldrew in *One Foot in the Grave*. He is also a highly acclaimed theatre director.

Barry Cryer is a comedy performer and writer who has written for, among others, *The Frost Report*, Les Dawson, Morecambe & Wise, Jack Benny and Kenny Everett.

Ray Galton & Alan Simpson created and wrote *Hancock's Half Hour* and *Steptoe and Son*, acclaimed as the first British sitcoms of the modern era.

Graham Linehan is the co-writer of *Father Ted* and the writer of *The IT Crowd*. Formerly, he has written for Steve Coogan, Alexi Sayle, and *The Fast Show*.

Andrew Sachs is best known as Manuel, the lovable but dim waiter in *Fawlty Towers*. He has acted on stage, TV, and radio, and voiced documentaries and talking books.

Nigel Planer is best known as Neil in *The Young Ones*, and spoof actor Nicholas Craig. He has written several novels and starred in many stage shows.

John Dunsworth played arguably the greatest TV drunk: Officer Jim Lahey, in *Trailer Park Boys*. He has a long and distinguished stage and TV portfolio.

***

Stan Laurel & Oliver Hardy – Some of the thoughts of the two men themselves are included from rare archive interviews.

1. Characters

The expression 'character comedy' is often used to describe a particular type of humour but in truth, all comedy is *character comedy*. You laugh more easily and more often among close friends than you would in any other situation. You know these characters so well that even the smallest unscripted moment can bring a smile to your face. In fact, it is a truism in writing that stories can grow only when there are interesting characters in which to seed them; the characters come first. So it was with Laurel and Hardy.

[Stan Laurel] *It was the two characters. With most of the teams, there was the straight man and the comic. With us, there were two comics…two characters.*

Stan Laurel used the word *character* often in interviews. He realised that you can unleash pails of water, pots of paint, chimneyfuls of soot, angry landlords, jealous wives and heavy-handed bailiffs and policemen on any two people, but it will not be funny if you don't believe in and care for those people.

[Bruce Forsyth] *The lovely thing about Laurel and Hardy is that I believed them. Their comedy was so pure that I could imagine two guys just like them.*

[Stephen Merchant] *You feel that you can relate to them. So many of the other names have fallen off the map because they don't have that truth behind them. Abbott and Costello are essentially a vaudeville act, and I think they are very good, but they don't have that realism; you don't really believe that they inhabit a world. But with Laurel and Hardy, you do, endlessly.*

[Barry Cryer] *Abbott and Costello were brilliant, particularly Lou Costello I have to say, but theirs was a bang, bang, bang, classical double act – feed line and then the funny man does the joke – but they had no depth. Laurel and Hardy had real character depth. And they also looked as if they liked each other, as men as* *well as performers. You got this warmth and felt that in the finish, Ollie would never betray Stan.*

[Ardal O'Hanlon] *They were such definite characters, very rounded. You could see a silhouette of Laurel and Hardy from a distance of a hundred yards, and they'd be instantly recognisable. They had a great image – so bold and strong.*

Laurel and Hardy were two characters that people, all over the world, recognised instantly and understood. When their familiar theme music, 'The Cuckoo Song,' started up, you knew exactly what was in store, and it excited not only a feeling of great familiarity but also of great warmth.

[Graham Linehan] *I'm not a huge fan of a lot of the stuff from the silent era. I admired many of the things that Chaplin and Keaton did but what you're really looking to do is just laugh uncontrollably, and Laurel and Hardy are still able to reach out from the past and make you do that.*

[Galton & Simpson] *The impression you get with Chaplin is that he was far too deliberate. He was brilliant in what he did but Laurel and Hardy seemed more natural.*

The obvious question is where did these two characters come from? Who dreamt up Stan and Ollie? Who plagued movie producers and studio executives with scripts, imploring them to give the idea a break? The truth is that there was no single creator; the Laurel and Hardy characters simply evolved, and it took quite some time.

The events that begot Stan and Ollie are often recounted but don't align into a single agreed story. Some people credit Leo McCarey, a supervisor at the Hal Roach Studios where Laurel and Hardy made most of their films (31 silent shorts, 40 talking shorts, and 14 feature films) with spotting and nurturing the rapport. Others credit Hal Roach, himself. Many argue that Stan Laurel – part actor, part writer, part editor, part producer – contributed more to forming the characters than anyone else. In truth, it was probably all of these people and quite a few more: writers, gag men, directors and even supporting actors. And it wasn't just people but also circumstance and environment that allowed the characters to grow. Principal among these environmental factors was the movie studio of Hal Roach.

The Hal Roach Studio provided the ideal climate for Laurel and Hardy in the mid-1920s. Big enough to employ quality actors, directors, writers, and technicians, it was not so large that films had to be made in the regimented way they were produced in the movie factories of Fox, Universal, and MGM. The studio facilitated quality without compromising creativity. Moreover, its sole business was laughter.

Stan Laurel had made a circuitous and at times torrid journey to Roach, where, at the age of 37, he was about to form the most famous comedy partnership in history. But there are two ironies about the pairing of Laurel and Hardy in 1926. The first is that, at the time, Stan had all but given up on acting.

[Stan Laurel] *I wasn't too successful as a comic. They told me my eyes were too blue to photograph, which was a kind excuse, and I didn't feel I was so hot myself. So I was very happy to get into some other end of the business. F. Richard Jones was the supervisor at Roach and he felt I had great possibilities as a director, so during this time they made a director out of me.*

Laurel was working on what was known as the *All-Star Comedies* which paired so-called fallen stars of silent cinema – Theda Barra, Lionel Barrymore, Agnes Ayers, Priscilla Dean – with members of a company of stock comic actors to make short films. Before the shooting of one such film, a cast member was hospitalised and, with no time to seek a replacement, Hal Roach suggested that Stan Laurel step in. But this wasn't the chance event that brought the team together because the second irony in this story is that the actor Stan replaced was Oliver Hardy.

The film, *Get 'Em Young*, however, did well in preview, and Roach persuaded Laurel to write himself into subsequent pictures. When Oliver Hardy – who had burnt himself badly while cooking a leg of lamb – returned to work, he and Stan found themselves sharing the screen. It took some time to spot the chemistry between the two actors but it is fascinating, in their early silent films, to watch this process taking place.

The opportunity to observe and then improve a sitcom is not offered to many in television in the modern era, but there are some famous examples.

[Tony Robinson] *At the end of the first* Blackadder *series, I think it was plain to all of us that Rowan's character was too much of a grotesque and not funny enough, and that in order for him to be funnier, he needed to have this enormous confidence in how clever he was. And he wouldn't be able to do this unless there were people who were more stupid than him. So it was decided to recreate Baldrick as the stupidest person who had ever lived.*

Most sitcoms don't undergo an about-turn of this sort but all take their time to bed down, and subtle changes in character are an integral part of the process. An actor playing a part is a little like a musician performing a cover version of a song. The actor's interpretation of the character as they come to read it in the script will be different to that of the writer, and the nuance and action they use to bring the character to life will go beyond what is written in the lines. Indeed, actors often use the term 'interpret' when referring to how they play a character. They read the script and *interpret* what kind of character would say those lines, and then they try to become that person.

Writers often talk about how, having observed the first incarnation of a character, they will write a slightly different version of that character for subsequent series. In many ways, it is a process of writing to the actor's observed strengths.

[Galton & Simpson] *When we first wrote for Tony Hancock, he had been playing a schoolmaster in* Educating Archie *and it was all a bit seedy and a bit Will Hay, 'Oh' and 'Yes, I see' and*

'My Word', etc. Gradually, we got him to play it as himself. It took a couple of years and even in the first Hancock's Half Hour *on television, which was about two years after we started working with him, he still had the leftovers of this character Archie. But in the end, we created a character in his image, and you wouldn't be able to tell the difference between the character and the actor, except, of course, that their attitude towards things was totally different.*

What is remarkable about Laurel and Hardy's first silent film together, *Duck Soup*, is not how different the two characters are to what they eventually became, but how similar. The development of their personas, it seems, wasn't a steady, assured convergence but rather a haphazard trial-and-error process. And, oddly, they were closer to the finished product in that very first film than they would be in the next eight or nine. (Incidentally it is not known who came up with the film's title, *Duck Soup*, but what is known is that the 1933 Marx Brothers movie of the same name was christened by its director, Leo McCarey – a former studio executive at the Roach Studios, a sometime director of Laurel and Hardy, and the person most usually credited with pairing the two comics in the first place.)

In *Duck Soup*, Laurel and Hardy play two hoboes who get chased into a mansion vacated by the owner, Colonel Blood, and realise that the butler and the maid have absconded for the weekend. So when a couple call to rent the house, Ollie pretends to be the proprietor and Stan dresses up as both butler and maid in quick clothes-swapping farce. Many people will recognise this as the plot of their later 1930 talking short, *Another Fine Mess*, and the similarities in plot are nearly matched by the similarities in character.

Ollie is the boss and has many of the plummy, pompous gestures for which he became famous. In one instance, he snatches a business card out of Stan's hand, points at his own chest and intimates that he will be the one to read it. In another, he makes great play of extricating a cigar from an inside pocket. Stan is probably less his final self than Ollie, but there is a moment when Ollie hides behind a curtain and Stan follows, only to be shoved out to find his own hiding place. It shows all the innocent, childish dependency that audiences came to love in Stan Laurel.

The main difference – apart from Ollie's top hat and stubble, Stan's Harold-Lloyd-like hand-to-face gesture and some highly improbable dialogue captions – is the speed at which things proceed. The way, in subsequent films, Laurel and Hardy slowed down the action and took time to react to what was happening, is probably their greatest single innovation. The pace in this early film, however, is uncharacteristically brisk, and a good deal more happens in this 20-minute film than in the 1930 remake which runs for half an hour. By and large, though, this is a close approximation to what would come, so why were these characterisations not nurtured from the off?

Maybe this shouldn't be surprising. In the same way that friends that make you laugh, now, probably didn't make you laugh the first time you met them, many comedies take time to catch on. *Only Fools and Horses* is one of the most famous examples. The first series, in 1981, met with a lukewarm response, but the show was lucky – by television standards – in receiving a second chance. However, when this subsequent series garnered only moderate approval, it looked like it would get the axe. It was only an upturn in viewing figures for summer repeats that encouraged the BBC to stick with what would become probably their most successful sitcom ever.

Minder is a more unusual case since it wasn't even intended to be a comedy. It was originally conceived as a fast-paced, dramatic vehicle for Dennis Waterman in the mould of *The Sweeney,* but it moved in a more comedic direction when the Arthur Daley character, played so brilliantly by George Cole, came alive on-screen.

For Laurel and Hardy over the next dozen or so films, the characters we now know so well flickered in and out of focus before, in the latter half of 1927, they became more or less stable. They continued to develop in subsequent pictures, but there was no backsliding, only a subtle paring, layering, and slowing. By the time sound arrived in 1929, Laurel and Hardy were famous worldwide and, fortunately, dialogue added a dimension to the characters without jarring against what had already evolved.

[Bruce Forsyth] *They gained even more when the talkies came along; it made them funnier. Now you could actually put voices to these two characters.*

However, despite the fact that Laurel and Hardy's debut sound film, *Unaccustomed As We Are* (1929), was one of the very first talking films to be released in Hollywood, Stan Laurel was smart enough not to be besotted by the innovation of sound and the characters that had been formed so meticulously over the last three years were never compromised.

[Stan Laurel] *I think we were fortunate in sticking to our silent reel methods when talkies came in. We only said enough to motivate what we were doing. Everybody started to talk their heads off for no reason at all. Line after line of dialogue; they were forgetting the principle of the comic for the sheer novelty of being able to talk on film. And a lot of them couldn't talk, like we couldn't talk. We weren't talking comedians, so our dialogue was very static.*

We used sound chiefly for the effects and after a while we really liked it because it emphasized the gags and, as time went on, we became a little more accustomed and did more talking than first intended.

If you watch one of the later silent films, like *Big Business* (1928) or *Angora Love* (1929), the characters you see are clearly identifiable as the characters audiences would come to hear the following year. Sound may have altered the Laurel and Hardy films for the better, but it didn't change their characters. So who were these two people? At various times policemen, road sweepers, soldiers, buskers, bandits, barbers, sailors, chimney-sweeps, Christmas tree salesmen, tramps, removals men, toymakers and, one occasion, oil magnates. They never changed. They may have been married, single, playing as their wives, or as their children, or even – briefly, in *Thicker Than Water* – as each other, but you could always see the same two characters. So what was so funny about them?

[Graham Linehan] *It's a nice match up really, an idiot who doesn't realise that he's an idiot and an idiot who kind of accepts that he's an idiot. The blind leading the blind.*

[Galton & Simpson] *It's a great comedy of attitudes. The classic comedy character is the fella who thinks he knows it all, whereas in fact he is as big an idiot as everybody else, which, in our work, is reflected in Hancock. Hardy fancies himself as a bit of a know-all, whereas you realise he knows no more than Laurel, which is a classic situation. It's exactly the same in* The Office.

[Barry Cryer] *Eric Morecambe defined him and Ernie brilliantly when he said, 'We're two idiots but I'm a bigger idiot than him because I think I'm smarter than him.' And Ollie was always under the illusion that he was a much more intelligent man than Stan and he was just as hopeless in any situation when it came down to it.*

It seems the Laurel and Hardy pairing is somehow archetypal. Stephen Merchant sees a thread that links David Brent in *The Office* with so many of the great sitcom antiheroes and which winds its way right back to Laurel and Hardy.

[Stephen Merchant] *One thing that we [myself and Ricky Gervais] are both very interested in, is the idea of 'lives of quiet desperation' where you are trapped in a world from which you cannot escape. And there is a disparity between the hopes and ambitions that you have for yourself and your inability to achieve them because of your own failings, be that a lack of education, or intelligence or even self-awareness. David Brent is a man with pretensions, constantly undone by his own idiocy. But the disparity between his ambitions and his actual ability are what make it funny, and you also see that* *in Fawlty, Hancock, Alan Partridge, even Woody Allen. And Oliver Hardy is the first of those classic comic characters on screen.*

[Andrew Sachs] *The contrasting physical shapes helps. Laurel and Hardy certainly had that and so did John [Cleese] and I. It's a typical setup, isn't it, two people who appear to be very different but are just as hopeless as each other.*

Even young children understand this archetype of grown-ups – parents, teachers, narky neighbours – who take themselves very seriously but, they can observe, are actually very stupid.

[Nigel Planer] *As a kid the idea of grown-ups being silly is obviously funny, but with Stan and Ollie there is the added implication of parental respectability because of their suits and ties and hats, and the way they try so hard to keep their dignity. They are not dressed as tramps nor as clowns. They are in uniforms often and are trying to do things which most adults manage perfectly well but they behave like children. It is like watching your own parents being silly which is a forbidden pleasure for children.*

Like all great characters, Stan and Ollie weren't the fruits of a logical process but just grew in the direction of the light of what was funny. And what allowed them to live and breathe and ultimately make us laugh were the situations in which they found themselves. For these characters to seem believable, they had to find themselves in a believable world, a meticulously constructed virtual reality that looked plausible for them. And the importance of these situations was as carefully respected by Laurel and Hardy then as it is by the sitcom writers of today.

[Graham Linehan] *What you're looking to do is to create a world that you can turn to again and again, knowing that there are certain rules that won't be broken so that it feels like these people are real. As with Laurel and Hardy, even though they've somehow been given all these jobs that they aren't really capable of, you do somehow believe that they could exist. But you need to create those rules, or it just doesn't feel like reality, it just feels like some silly writers sat down and made up a lot of stuff.*

This idea of putting interesting characters into difficult situations and watching them spark off one another is the mainstay of all sitcoms, and when done well it can even do away with the need for jokes. Think of the squabbles in *The Royal Family*, *The Office*, *The Young Ones*, or *Steptoe & Son*; it's the characters reacting to adversity and each other that makes you laugh. The words become tied in with the characters and are funny because of this, not because they are necessarily jokes in their own right. The character placed into the situation is what generates the laugh.

[Tony Robinson] *Every second-rate comic wants to be the funniest person in the show, whereas every first-rate comic wants to be occupying the funniest possible world that he can, surrounding him- or herself with quality performers.*

It was this idea – of the comedy arising out of the situations, rather than by any one funny joker within that situation – that probably best explains the Laurel and Hardy approach to characterisation. Oliver Hardy, in a rare soundbite, expressed this himself.

[Oliver Hardy] *Hundreds of stories have been submitted to us that we've been compelled to turn down. Not that they haven't sufficient elements of comedy but because they don't fit the characters that we have established as fundamentally ours.*

In order to do this believably, both Stan Laurel and Oliver Hardy had to be first-rate actors. Although Laurel came from a stage background and made several attempts to succeed as a solo comedian, in the Laurel and Hardy films he never seeks laughs on his own account and always plays faithfully, and in a very understated way, to character. So too Oliver Hardy, who was acting in front of a camera from the age of 21 and never performed on stage.

It is strange, then, that this lesson had to be learned again in the early days of television comedy, when it was comedians rather than actors who played the lead roles and usually trampled the boundaries of the situations in which they appeared by allowing their comic personas to gush to the surface. *Steptoe & Son* is often credited as the first comedy to buck this trend as the writers cast recognised straight actors, Harry H. Corbett and Wilfrid Brambell, in the lead roles. Even before *Steptoe*, they were moving in this direction.

[Galton & Simpson] *We wanted to work with actors instead of comedians, and we started using more and more actors in* Hancock. *And it worked very well as Tony required authenticity to play against and was so much better working off straight actors. Of course, you had to have actors who had a sense of humour but what you didn't want was people 'being funny'. And whenever you got comedy characters like Dick Emery, their instinct is to ham it up. Dick Emery never played anything as himself – it was always funny voices and funny moves – but with Tony you wanted someone who was genuine and straight. So we decided to try and get away from funny men and let the characters speak to get the humour out of the characters and the situations.*

Andrew Sachs learnt this lesson – serving the character instead of seeking laughs directly – through many years of experience.

[Andrew Sachs] *What I do is character acting, really, rather than pure comedy. I wouldn't say I was a specialist comedy actor, and it took me a long time to learn this. When I was doing farce with Brian Rix at the Whitehall Theatre, we had to be funny to satisfy an audience who demanded it. So if I was given the part of a character, I would say, 'How can I make him funny?' I'd do it in a funny accent or with a limp or I'd fall down, and I made a lot of mistakes that way. That's not the way to play comedy for me; it's a lesson I've learnt.*

Laurel and Hardy, the actors, knew Laurel and Hardy the characters and portrayed them with integrity, so the world they inhabited was believable. (The reason they used their real names, incidentally, is that the studio held the rights to the names of characters – Hickory Hiram was one of Stan's during a short stint with Universal – and could retain these monikers even if the stars that played them moved on. However, they couldn't claim possession of Stan and Ollie's real names.) And it doesn't matter that their world seems slightly slippier, or slightly sootier, or slightly more treacherous than our own, because of the way the characters acted within it, we knew that this world was real.

[Richard Wilson] *I'm saddled by this catchphrase 'I don't believe it,' but before I did Victor, when directing actors on stage, I always talked about 'believability.' The audience has to believe what the people are saying and to do that, the actors have to believe and know who they are. So I'm always trying to get my actors to be honest. There's a lot of acting that goes on that is really nothing to do with the character and more to do with the actor, and I don't like that. Laurel and Hardy just seemed to know exactly who they were and let us watch them. And it was a privilege.*

2. Stan

Surprisingly, in the Laurel and Hardy team, Stan was the brains. Oliver Hardy arrived punctually, worked hard and left at five. Stan Laurel, on the other hand, from the time he watched the rushes in the morning until the time he left the Culver City studio long after dark, was a writer, gagman, director, actor and even editor.

Many people in the performing professions hail from performing families and so it was with Stan Laurel. His father, Arthur Jefferson, or 'A.J.' as he was known, managed several theatres and theatre companies in the north of England and wrote, produced and acted in many plays. His mother, Madge, was a beautiful actress with a trained mezzo singing voice.

Stan was born on 16 June 1890, in Ulverston, Lancashire, a small seaside town south of the Lake District. He was christened Arthur Stanley Jefferson and, from an early age, longed to follow in his parents' footsteps.

Although Stan was always involved with comedy, and although it could be said that laughter was in his blood, it is not certain that his sole instinct was to make people laugh in the yearning, often self-absorbed way that many comedians approach the profession. His own recollections suggest more chance in his choice of speciality.

[Stan Laurel] *I had quite a lisp at that time and my voice was kind of broken and I was just ill-fitted for anything but a comic. So I decided that that was my forte.*

Given that he later accepted his limitations (perceived limitations, that is) as a performer and had resolved to make a fist of it behind the camera, it might be truer to say that Stan Laurel was always committed to working on something that ultimately made people laugh, rather than on necessarily needing to be the funny man himself.

His career path was a meandering one and most remarkable about the 16-year period following his first trip to the US in 1910 is the seeming lack of progress. Certainly he was learning valuable lessons in that time but there is little outward sign that these were causing his star to rise. And, in later interviews, there is scant mention of his inner thoughts during the purgatory where he dreamed of making it big without knowing if he ever would.

On that first trip to the US, he had been understudy to – of all people – Charlie Chaplin, in the Fred Karno music-hall troupe. The two comics even roomed together for one brief spell in a drafty squat off Times Square but when Chaplin left to make films for Mack Sennett, the show ran aground and Stan was forced to return to England. He was involved with a doomed tour of northern Europe before sailing a second time for the United States in 1912. He picked up several jobs in film but worked mostly on stage in vaudeville. One thing that he did come to realise in this period was that he performed better with others than he did on his own.

[Stan Laurel] *I was never successful in solo work. I always had to have a foil.*

He also changed his name from Stan Jefferson to Stan Laurel.

[Stan Laurel] *I changed the name on account of billing. You see Jefferson was quite a long name, so it always appeared small on the billing on that account. So I thought if I had a shorter name, the letters would be bigger* [laughing]. *I don't know where the Laurel came from.*

In this time, Stan was moderately successful and managed to get by but given the arduous nature of the work – in theatre, particularly – it wasn't a glamorous lifestyle. It seems, in all of this, that Stan was useful without being remarkable but it also shows something else: he was driven.

By the time he returned to the Hal Roach studios in 1926 (he had made a series of five comedy shorts in a brief, unremarkable stint there in 1918), he did at least have talents that people at the studio felt were worth nurturing. He may not have been much nearer to his on-screen character but he had learnt a lot about the business that would eventually help him to bring this character, along with Oliver Hardy's, to life.

Regarding Stan's various on-screen guises up to this point, it is difficult to say anything very positive. All were somehow sub-Chaplin, with an unconvincing mixture of vulnerability and quick-limbed cleverness, but none possessed a persona you could feel for. Stan was never very believable, funny or likeable when he was leading the action and this he had to do when starring on his own. What he really needed was somebody to work off – somebody to tell him what to do, to introduce him to strangers and ultimately to exasperate.

When he did finally find this place next to Oliver Hardy – his partner professionally for the next 30 years and his pal, on-screen, for life – he was able, slowly, to breathe life into a character that would become the inspiration for many comic actors to follow.

[Ardal O'Hanlon] *I absorbed such a lot from what Stan Laurel was doing, which is inevitable, really, if you're playing a dumb sidekick because he is the archetype; he is the grandfather of dumb sidekicks. In hindsight, I was almost slightly ashamed at how clearly inspired and influenced by Laurel and Hardy we all were on the* Father Ted *project but it was all subliminal in my case as I hadn't actually watched Laurel and Hardy for a good ten or 15 years before that. Also, because I was working from a position of ignorance, as I was very much a stand-up going into this whole sitcom territory, I was kind of making it up as I went along, blindly. It's only looking back that you realise, yes, I was very influenced by him.*

[Tony Robinson] *I think it would be wrong to say that any actor models their performance on another performance or what you do* *is simply going to be derivative. But I was certainly inspired by Stan Laurel's work. He had such great facial economy and yet he was able to put over this appealing and put-upon guy and consequently he was very much one of my influences when I created Baldrick. I wanted this notion of a character who was down-trodden but didn't whinge and express his piteousness. He was just there and the audience could fill in the emotions.*

This contentment and self-containment seems to be a key feature in making the characters of Stan, Dougal and Baldrick work, and it is a trait shared by another famous, lovable dimwit.

[Andrew Sachs] *Manuel is the only happy one in* Fawlty Towers. *He feels at home; it's a new family for him. And when he gets hit or is abused by the boss, in a way, this takes him back to childhood when he was – and I invented this for myself – probably one of ten children where the only way to be noticed is to be different. If you get a clip around the ear hole, it means that somebody is concerned about you. So he takes it all as part of everyday life and he loves it. The Fawltys are another family for Manuel, in Britain.*

There was a certain blank passivity that formed an integral part of Stan's character. Quite often it was his hesitancy or simple blank confusion that got the laugh.

[Graham Linehan] *I notice that Stan, in particular, doesn't move a lot, unless he has done something wrong. A lot of the time everybody else is fluttering around the two of them, issuing commands, getting angry, shouting, threatening them, while they just stand there. And then Stan would turn and whack someone on the face with something, which in a way is almost a kind of revenge on the people in the talkies by two guys who started off in silent movies.*

Stan Laurel deliberately aimed for this blank look. He wore light make-up and made sure that the shots were lit in such a way as to rub out lines and facial definition. He used to say to perennial cameraman, Art Lloyd, 'Wash me out, Artie; no shadows. I want to be flat-faced.' Art Lloyd, to his frustration, was never allowed to do anything artistic with the photography owing to the bright lighting that bathed all parts of the set.

But this lighting served the comedy in other ways. Not only did it make the scenes seem sunny and more conducive to laughter, but with the set lit evenly, the actors were always covered if they improvised or decided at short notice (as they often did) to take the action in a different direction. And despite the simplifying of Stan's facial definition, there was no softness to his character definition.

[Richard Wilson] *Stan has got this vulnerability, this extraordinary openness. I think he is the great one of the two. Oliver Hardy is just the perfect foil for him, although it always seems the other way around. But to me it's Stan Laurel who's the genius. I always look upon him as the real actor, somehow.*

Although comic characters may seem very far from the comic actors that play them, there are usually many similarities. Often the character is an exaggerated or warped version of the actor – the person, in extremis, that the player might have turned out to be – and this inner knowledge of the character helps to make them seem real. In this regard, Stan Laurel's 16-year apprenticeship in the US might have fed into his humble screen persona. There was a grounded humanity in Stan Laurel that he probably inherited from his father.

[Stan Laurel] *[My father] was charitable to the poor, giving shoes and stockings to poor kids who couldn't afford them. He also arranged special matinees many times for the inmates of the poorhouses. He'd pick them up in buses, and when they left the show, he gave them all packages of tea, sugar, cookies, tobacco, and snuff. He liked everybody and everybody liked him. I think that's why he was such a good showman.*

This sense of sympathy, humility and accessibility seems to have passed from father to son, and, with it, maybe something else. Stan didn't live with his parents for the first five years of his life. Instead, he was brought up by his grandmother on his mother's side, and his alcoholic grandfather. His mother was too ill to look after her own children during this time and his father had a reputation as a philanderer. This must all, surely, have upset the foundations of those important early years and this vulnerability could have been tapped into, however subliminally, when Arthur Stan Jefferson came to play Stan. Comedians often draw on their deepest subconscious obsessions when creating a comedy persona.

[Nigel Planer] *You create a persona that comes from an exaggerated version of yourself, and in my case Neil from* The Young Ones *would definitely fit into that category, as would Nicholas Craig. That would also apply to people like Fawlty or Ricky Gervais's character. When you are trying to find out how to make people laugh, you must take into account your own personality and physique…your type. Groucho being vulnerable or sweet? No. Your clown will come from you and you have to find your own clown. Is it a sad clown, is it a happy one, or whatever?*

[Ardal O'Hanlon] *I think the writers [of* Father Ted*] were quite astute. They felt that what I was doing in stand-up would be quite suitable for their character Dougal. Where that persona came from originally, I'm nearly afraid to explore. I think it emanates from a real reluctance to get on stage in the first place and a defence mechanism. I actually* was *a frightened rabbit on the stage, so I just played into it. It seemed to make sense to go with it, rather than pretending I'm something I'm not…like a strong, confident, opinionated person.*

[Andrew Sachs] *I think there must be some of me in Manuel. I'm a bit of a peace-maker, wherever possible, and I accept life as it comes and I'm certain Manuel is similar. He doesn't really like arguments and he's always willing to help; he would make a marvellous father and husband. He's much nicer than me. I think Manuel is actually a bit of a hero of mine.*

When looking at the roots of character, it is interesting to compare Stan Laurel's upbringing to that of Charlie Chaplin. Although Stan Laurel's childhood was a little footless, Chaplin's was hugely turbulent. His alcoholic father died when he was only 12, his mother was institutionalised and Chaplin himself, as a child, spent some time in the poorhouse. He was, however, resolutely determined to make good of himself. From the moment he hit American soil, he was on the up. He gained full creative control of every film he made from 1918 onwards and in his films, which frequently revisited scenes from his youth, Chaplin's Tramp character is penniless and put-upon but smarter than everybody he encounters and ultimately triumphant. Surely this reflects a lot about Charlie Chaplin's personal struggles and consequent ambition.

Stan Laurel's on-screen character, by comparison, is far less assertive but, when left to his own devices, content. It is only when he is forced to engage with the outside world that Stan becomes confused or upset.

One of the most endearing portraits of Stan's character comes in *County Hospital* (1932). Visiting his sick friend – Ollie, in a comically enormous leg-cast – Stan spends the first few minutes of this film trying to navigate his way to Ollie's room on the top floor. At reception, he says simply, 'I'd like to see Mr Hardy,' and then leaning over the counter to view the register the nurse is checking, adds, 'Oliver Norvell Hardy,' in the way he has so often seen his companion do. When the nurse tells him that Mr Hardy is in a room 'next to the solarium,' Stan is obviously baffled, but he doesn't say anything. He internalises the notion for a few seconds, then leans over the counter a second time, then thinks on this a little more, before finally throwing up his arms and walking on.

It is charming to observe this wariness in Stan's demeanour. His experience of a gruff and cynical world has led him to keep out of people's way where possible, and yet nearly everything that goes wrong in *County Hospital*, goes wrong because of Stan. His pompous, oftentimes dumber, friend Ollie is, in this film, pretty near blameless.

Over the decades, the vulnerability of Stan's on-screen character seems to have won it the popular vote over Charlie Chaplin's tramp, but it should be pointed out that Stan Laurel's respect for his one-time room-mate was absolute.

[Stan Laurel] *He could have them laughing one minute and crying the next – the lump in the throat. That's a great artist, I think. With the audiences he was sure-fire every time.*

I don't think there's any greater in the business or ever will be. He's the greatest artist that was ever on the screen. In real life I only knew him when we were together in the old days in vaudeville. He was just a regular guy and I always found him quite pleasant.

It is impossible, as a last word in this chapter, not to say something about Stan Laurel's personal life. There are a number of good biographies which document his personal affairs in great detail, but even reading these, you're left to reflect that it is so difficult, and ultimately pointless, to try to *sum up* any one person's life. From all that I have read, I feel qualified to mention only two things.

The first is about his home life. He had four wives, although, bizarrely, he was married five times, as he remarried second wife Ruth after his third marriage broke up. It is often said that he was a philanderer but this is not the case. No philanderer with any dedication to his vice would get married five times. Stan Laurel was, in fact, a highly principled man, who fell uncontrollably in love with women at different times in his life and married every one. The problems, it seems, started when things settled into the normality of family life. Although it is true to say that some of Stan Laurel's wives were 'difficult,' he himself was somehow detached at home. (He also had had a son, Stanley Robert, who was born prematurely in 1930 but died nine days later.) Maybe it was the unstable family roots from which he sprang but Stan never seemed to build anything solid in any of these marriages, except perhaps in his last, to Ida, with whom he stayed until he died in 1965. Stan Laurel's only long-standing commitment was to making films but, as he reflected late in his life, 'I'm sure nothing I did was very amusing to any of my wives.'

These words bring me to the second thing I feel should be said about Stan Laurel. There can be no doubt from all that is written, from the accounts of people who worked with him and met him, and even from the interviews that Stan Laurel himself gave, that he was, notwithstanding world fame and unprecedented public affection, an incredibly modest and grounded person. He entertained no sense of himself as a genius or someone who was in any way better than anybody else. He was polite and patient with everyone, laughing generously with the same whooping high-pitched laugh that his screen-character used. When asked about the enormous popularity his films were still enjoying in cinemas all over Europe three decades after they were made, he answered simply, 'I frankly don't know, I really don't. It's amazing.'

Stan Laurel made a point of answering every piece of fan mail that was sent to him. Incredibly, after he retired, you could find his name in the regular Los Angeles telephone directory, and many people phoned him and called out to his Santa Monica apartment to ask him about his life and his films. According to his last wife, Ida, as well as numerous people that visited, Stan would entertain these guests graciously and patiently. And this modesty and unassuming accessibility was something he shared with his comedy partner.

3. Oliver Norvell Hardy

[Oliver Hardy] *There's very little to say. Stan can fill you in on all the comedy stuff in the pictures. As for my life, it wasn't very exciting, and I didn't do very much outside of doing a lot of gags before a camera and playing golf the rest of the time.*

This lack of conceit is echoed in many stories told about both Oliver Hardy and Stan Laurel.

[Barry Cryer] *Ray Allen, the ventriloquist, was on the bill with them [in their UK stage tour of 1953] and he said they were so courteous and polite with the rest of the cast. He was overawed by them but he finally summoned up a bit of courage and asked for a signed photograph. Oliver Hardy said, 'Certainly,' but two days went by and nothing happened and Ray thought, oh dear, I won't mention it again. Then he was in his dressing room, which was way up at the top of the theatre, and he heard these footsteps clumping up the stairs and it was Ollie, coming all the way up to* his *dressing room to give him the photograph. He wasn't summoned to* their *dressing room and Ray Allen said he would never forget that. I never heard a bad word about them from anybody who ever worked with or met them.*

Amazingly, Oliver Hardy thought of himself, more or less, as the straight man. In his mind, he was just there to facilitate the comedy that Stan Laurel was creating. This tallies with the idea, already expressed, that the humour in these films comes from the situations as played by the actors, not directly from the comedians themselves, but for Oliver Hardy to think that he wasn't particularly funny seems incredible.

[Bruce Forsyth] *What I loved about them was they were both funny. It wasn't that one was the straight man and one was funny; they were both hysterical.*

Oliver Hardy shares his most endearing comic trait with Bruce Forsyth – namely his ability to bring the audience into the action with even the slightest look to camera. This seems a simple device and yet very few people have been able to use it with the subtlety that Oliver Hardy first did almost eight decades ago.

[Bruce Forsyth] *I think Oliver Hardy made me aware of it, more than anybody else…treating the camera as a person, as the third party in the conversation. So later on, maybe, that's what made me think the camera is so important when you're working on television or in film. I often do it when I'm being interviewed. I'd talk to the person – which you have to do when you're doing an interview – but then if I had a little aside to the camera, it brings the audience in and lets them know that they are there, in the same way that Oliver Hardy used to do.*

Interestingly, Oliver Hardy's and Bruce Forsyth's development of this relationship with the viewer happened in very different settings, which suggests that it comes more from the personality and disposition of the performer than from anything external. Oliver Hardy worked solely in film, and never – except to sing in cabaret, on a few occasions – took to the stage, whereas Bruce Forsyth's desire to involve the audience stemmed directly from his stage background.

[Bruce Forsyth] *I was doing theatre work mostly before I did anything on television, and of course in the theatre you just work to your audience, so your eyes and your eye line would be anywhere from the top of the gallery, to the dress circle, to different parts of the stalls; you have to encompass the whole audience in your performance. In* The Generation Game *and* Play Your Cards Right, *I had what was called a slave camera. It was my camera, my slave, that I knew was always on me whenever I was working, the whole way through the show. And I would refer to it at certain times when I wanted to do an intimate bit, full into that special camera. Now you have about six cameras, whereas in the old days there'd only be one or two.*

The problem of multiple camera angles was not one that troubled Oliver Hardy, however, because of the way Stan Laurel engineered most of the shots. He wanted the laughs to come out of the performance and not the cinematic technique and, to that end, a broad, still camera angle was usually preferred, so that the action approximated live theatre. In many ways, then, Stan was bringing the filming back to his own theatrical background in the same way that it would have worked for Bruce Forsyth, which made it easier for Oliver Hardy to know where the audience was at all times. And with this audience contact, Hardy was able to ground the oftentimes crazy action with very humane exasperation.

[Ardal O'Hanlon] *You need someone fairly normal at the centre of it all, which is definitely true in* Father Ted. *Ted is the only really rounded character. He's got a normal person's concerns and a normal person's foibles. He's vain, ambitious, grasping and frustrated.*

Ollie may be vain, pompous and deluded, but he is still slightly smarter than Stan and particularly funny are the occasions when things – even by the pair's normal standards – go really badly wrong, and Ollie displays what can only be described as exasperation beyond exasperation.

The 1933 short, *Dirty Work*, is just such an instance. Stan and Ollie arrive at the home of Professor Noodle to sweep his chimney. But you get the impression that whatever job they have come from hasn't gone well because, at the first sign of trouble, Ollie takes himself up to the roof, declaring to Stan, 'I'm going to stay as far away from you as possible.'

Dirty Work is one of Laurel and Hardy's really great short films. The pacing of débâcle and counter-débâcle is perfect and at the centre of the action, Oliver Hardy gives probably his most brilliantly infuriated performance ever. At each step in the soot-filled farce, he looks to the viewer as if to say, 'I'm really not in the mood for this.'

[Stephen Merchant] *There is a realism to the Laurel and Hardy relationship, and to their ambitions, that isn't just born out of comic convenience. There's a sort of sophistication to it and a truth,* *particularly Oliver Hardy. That persona is so sophisticated…the southern gent…the movements of the hand, the very specific and immaculate way he has of removing his hat and holding it under his arm and all these little gentlemanly flourishes. Even if they're homeless or on the breadline, he's still got pretensions, he still believes that he belongs in a better world.*

Like all great actors, Oliver Hardy developed these beautiful movements through observation. From a very early age, in the hotel his mother ran in Madison, Georgia, he engaged in a practice he continued throughout his life which he referred to as 'lobby watching.'

[Oliver Hardy] *I sit in the lobby and I watch people. I like to watch people. Once in a while, someone will ask me where Stan and I dreamed up the characters that we play in the movies. They seem to think that these two fellows aren't like anybody else. I know they're dumber than anyone else, but there are plenty of Laurels and Hardys in the world. Whenever I travel, I am still in the habit of sitting in the lobby and watching the people walk by – and I tell you I see many Laurels and Hardys.*

Not only were Hardy's actions a joy to behold for their own sake but they added to the humour of the situation in a unique way.

[Stephen Merchant] *One of the things you see in someone like Oliver Hardy is a tremendous precision in the way he uses his body. Nothing goes to waste. It's like with a mime, if you're flapping about it looks ungainly and ungracious, and likewise in modern comedy, there's something about being precise with your actions that somehow makes things funnier, or makes it a bit more clear in people's minds. I'm ashamed to admit that I'm not much of an actor but if I'm doing anything physical, I try, if I can, to make it quite precise as I think that makes it funnier.*

[Galton & Simpson] *Ollie has very delicate movements. For a big man. He dances, almost as if he had tiny feet and his hands are so very genteel.*

Ollie's grace and poise add a beautiful twist to his character but this aspect had rarely featured in the parts that he played before he was teamed with Stan Laurel. His stock role in pictures up to that point was the bushy-eyebrowed, moustached 'heavy' who featured in so many of the early silent films. Because of his size, Oliver Hardy was destined to fill this role from an early age.

He was born in Harlem, Georgia, on 18 January 1892. His father, a lawyer, died when he was an infant, and his mother ran the hotel where he first observed the ghosts of his future character. Unlike the Laurels, there was no show business in the Hardy family although there was a great love of music and he became a boy tenor, a schooling he drew on frequently on screen. He was christened 'Oliver Norvell Hardy,' the 'Norvell' being his mother's surname, and he used this extended title in films often.

[Oliver Hardy] *I use it in full, sometimes, when I want to sound very impressive. There's something about a three-barreled name that sounds impressive and, besides, I think my name does sound impressive. I like the sound of it and one thing I want to emphasise: I never use my name to make fun of it. I'm proud of my name, all of it.*

His academic career, like Stan's, was unremarkable, although he did train to be a lawyer for a short time at Columbia University. At the age of 18, he opened the first movie theatre in Milledgeville, Georgia, where the family had moved. Although details about this venture are scant, Hardy did say that the actors he observed in those early silent comedies inspired his next career move since he felt he could do as well them, at least, if not a great deal better. This prompted him to move to Jacksonville, Florida, where he got work in pictures at both the Lubin and Vim film studios.

It was in Jacksonville that he picked up his nickname, 'Babe,' from an Italian barber who took a shine to the cherubic actor, and who would pat his cheeks affectionately, saying, 'nice-a bab-ee, nice-a bab-ee.' Everyone called Oliver Hardy 'Babe' and there are actually a few moments in some of the silent films where Stan can be seen mouthing the word 'Babe.' In particular, in *Big Business* (1928), when he thinks he has secured an order for a Christmas tree from James Finlayson, you can clearly see Stan calling his partner back with this nickname.

Babe Hardy moved between New York and Jacksonville, all the time gaining credibility, before heading to Vitagraph in Hollywood in 1918. He worked with a number of studios prior to teaming up with Stan Laurel at Roach. However, their paths did cross once before in a film that Hardy made for Bronco Billy Anderson in 1919. In this two-reel short, both actors played to their types of the time: Babe, a gun-toting heavy; Stan, a guileless, albeit acrobatic innocent. The scene in which they meet and in which Hardy barks out the line, 'Put 'em both up, insect, before I comb your hair with lead,' is hard to watch objectively when you know everything that will follow. It's such an obvious squaring-up of the double-act-to-be with a small premonitory frisson added by the movie's title, *Lucky Dog*.

When they did team up, Hardy confined his efforts to acting and acting only. He rarely made suggestions on-set and trusted Stan's instincts in all things. Unlike Stan, he had a rich life outside films: he gardened, he cooked, he sang, he socialised, he went to the races, he played cards, he spectated at sporting events. But, more than any of these things, he golfed. He would hurry away at the end of a day's shooting to catch the last of the light on the nearby Lakeside golf course where he was a member, and he was so good that the annual Roach-studio golf outing was, reportedly, hardly worth staging if Babe Hardy took part.

But despite his passivity in the creative department, the odd suggestion that Oliver Hardy did proffer was always entertained and was invariably bang on. There was no competition between himself and Stan, and neither tried to steal a scene from the other. Hardy always turned up for work, he was fully prepared for the day's shooting, he never complained, he was utterly professional. Hal Roach recalled that he never heard Stan Laurel direct Oliver Hardy in anything, 'There was no need,' he said, 'since Hardy was such a good actor.'

Oliver Hardy was married three times but had no children. His third wife, Lucille, seems to have been his true love. She said of her husband that he was gracious and polite at all times. He was timid, sentimental, and sensitive, but was sure in his views and at times stubborn. He could lose his temper, but he never held a grudge. He looked after his friends as best he could and was, at all times, a gentleman.

Probably Babe Hardy's greatest contribution to the Laurel and Hardy films was the incredible intimacy he forged with the viewer, and the delicacy and deftness of a really great comic actor.

[Richard Wilson] *One of the things that is enjoyable about acting on camera is that you can, at times, take everything right down and the camera will capture it for you. There is a thrill in doing something that might not be at all spectacular but you think, yes, that's real…that is what that man would do. It gives you a great buzz sometimes, even though it's very simple.*

Oliver 'Babe' Hardy was a master of this seemingly 'very simple' craft.

4. Space

One of the greatest innovations of the Laurel and Hardy films was the way the action was slowed and time was allowed for the characters to react to what had happened. This was developed gradually during Laurel and Hardy's silent-film period and was driven, like everything else, by considerations of character. For if our heroes are two very dim people then it would be uncharacteristic of them to do anything quickly.

[Stan Laurel] *We slowed down in our shooting, in the speed of the film. They used to shoot at twelve [frames per second], so we went to normal…to fifteen or sixteen. We acted normally and stopped to show the reactions. Usually, in those days, they would take a pie in the face and then jump up and run and make funny gestures, whereas we got our pie and then deliberately stopped so you could read the man's thoughts.*

This slowness went very much against the fashion in film-making at the time but even by modern standards, the extent to which they take time to think about what they're going to do, and then react to what they have just done, is remarkable. There's a bravery about the comedy, a belief that it will be funny if it is given the space to breathe.

And it is not just the speed at which they do things which is brave but also the things they choose to do. Laurel and Hardy spun beautifully unhurried routines out of the simplest ideas. Take, for example, the famous scene in *Beau Hunks* (1931), where, after a day-long march in the desert, a weary Oliver Hardy removes what he thinks is his own boot and then slowly and meticulously rubs Stan's foot.

[Stephen Merchant] *It's such a brilliant idea, it's inspired, to spend so long massaging the wrong man's foot. It's completely surreal and yet also, somehow, completely believable. Absurd. And the slower they do it, the funnier it is.*

Even though modern comedy is mostly verbal rather than visual, the same principle applies. The viewer is interested in the characters and needs time to watch them and read their thoughts. But in a desire to serve the joke, scriptwriters can often lose sight of this.

[Ardal O'Hanlon] *In the first series of* Father Ted *we had a producer who really gave us a lot of license until we found our feet. He would encourage us to play and leave a shot just a little bit longer to put a bit more emphasis on reactions. But when I got to something like* My Hero, *there was no time for that. It was just bang, bang, bang…move it along, because there was a lack of faith in the material, I think, and in the characters, which is a shame.*

I remember seeing a clip of Some Mothers Do 'Ave 'Em *on one of those nostalgia shows, once, where I had to pick my favourite TV programmes, and there was a reaction that lasted a good minute. We timed it. Frank Spencer was just scratching his chin and looking at the audience and milking it for all it was worth. It's amazing what you can do when you're allowed to do it. It doesn't always have to be on the page. In fact, it's often the bits that aren't on the page that are most interesting. It's colouring in, or providing some little detail…it's the stuff that you can't actually really script at all. People should have a bit more faith in the actors. They've cast them, after all, so why not let them do what they do?*

For this process to work, everybody must be tuned into it. The writers have to write these pauses into the script, or allow for them, at least; the actors need the insight and confidence to carry them off and, most importantly, the producers and directors must trust both the writers and performers to do this.

[Graham Linehan] *It's something I'm always trying to get across to everybody I work with, especially actors. Actors can sometimes read a script and notice that they don't have any lines, but what they don't notice, very often, is that in the entire scene, all the big laughs will be when the camera cuts to them. In fact, if you look at Laurel and Hardy, a lot of the time they're the quietest people in the shot.*

It's a case of 'less is more,' and Andrew Sachs adopts an extreme form of minimalist performance in regard to the voiceovers he does for documentaries.

[Andrew Sachs] *If I ask somebody if they enjoyed a programme I'd narrated and they say, 'I didn't know there was a narration,' then that's the best compliment I can get. It doesn't happen often, but it has happened once or twice and when it does I'm very pleased with myself. You have to try and stamp on your own ego and not 'give a performance' but instead be truthful to the writer and the whole feel of the documentary. Put yourself in the background and if people hardly notice that you're doing a narration, then that's the best of all.*

The 1932 short *Towed in a Hole* contains a beautiful example of a long, silent reaction. Ollie is painting the rudder of their newly purchased boat while Stan scrubs the deck. At one point, Stan moves the tiller out of his way, with obvious consequences for Ollie below. When Ollie appears covered in paint, Stan immediately fears that he may have done something wrong. There follows a silent sequence where Stan stares at Ollie in confusion and trepidation from different vantages around the boat, eventually breaking the tense silence with the line, 'What did you put that stuff on your face for?' What is interesting about this is that the time between when the accident happens and Stan speaks is just over 60 seconds. Very few comedies would wait this long between two beats in a scene.

With Laurel and Hardy, there were so many examples of scenes built around small, seemingly silly ideas, but they were done so patiently and acted so believably, that they worked. For example, in several films – *Fra Diavolo*, *Them Thar Hills* and *Blotto* among them – they work a routine whereby a tipsy Stan gets a fit of the giggles. At first, Ollie is irritated, as people often are when watching someone else in hysterics, but bit by bit he gets sucked into the spirit of the moment and is eventually laughing uncontrollably himself.

As this situation builds, the audience watching the film start to smile and then chuckle and then laugh out loud as well. Incredibly, the first time Laurel and Hardy did this was in *Leave 'Em Laughing*, a silent film. It is one of those singular comic ideas which leaves you asking two questions. First, who would think of doing this? And, second, who would have the nerve to try to pull it off?

It helps, of course, if everyone involved is on the same wavelength and this was certainly the case at the Hal Roach Studios. Actors, writers, gagmen, directors, studio supervisors, and Hal Roach himself, were all aware of, and contributed to, the special method of film-making. Understanding between the different parties can be a great help to any project.

[Richard Wilson] *The only input I had to the script [of* One Foot in the Grave*] was in trying to get David [Renwick] to cut it. We would be forced to cut in the end because of timing within each episode. But I was always saying to him to let the scripts breathe a bit more, because the danger with cutting is that if you do it here and there, things become bitty. Whereas it's better if you let it flow from the very beginning and trust your material a bit more. I tried to persuade him to write less so that we didn't have to cut. Actors don't mind losing lines if it makes the thing better.*

Audiences need time to react or simply to enjoy what has just happened. By introducing the next gag too quickly, you're essentially competing with your own material, and the overall effect is reduced. If the actors are good – or, more to the point, if the *characters* are good – the audience will enjoy being in their company and will often laugh at times other than the obvious punctuations in the script.

[Richard Wilson] *When I'm directing, I don't think it's my job to say that I want a laugh here or anything like that. I always say, if you're doing your job properly, you'll get different laughs each night.*

I'm always on to my actors about being open…about opening out to the character and serving the character. And I find that Stan has got this extraordinary openness, somehow – you can see into his thinking.

He can tell you what he thinks with the raising of an eyebrow; it's extraordinarily subtle. I love the idea that the audience are invited to eavesdrop – they should be wanting to lean into the actors to find out what's going on. I don't like it when it's full on. I want the audience to do a bit of work.

This does seem to touch on some of the strange appeal of Laurel and Hardy. By doing less, they somehow expressed more. When Ollie, who is usually far more effusive than Stan, looks into the camera, although he's expressing his frustration, he's doing so by appealing to you. He's asking you, the viewer, to agree with him. He's saying, 'Did you see that? Wasn't that unbelievable? Wasn't it?' It's a very direct form of *openness*. And the passivity of Stan's expression works in the same way, without robbing him of character or making him any less interesting to the viewer.

Indeed, Stan Laurel actively sought this blank look, not only by getting the cameraman to 'wash him out,' as mentioned earlier, but also by using a light make-up and by lining the inner lids of his eyes to make them appear smaller. It seems a counter-intuitive approach for any actor to take but maybe it has its roots in something timeless.

[Tony Robinson] *What he was doing went right back to the beginning of performance, I think. Years ago, I was in the National Theatre, and I was working on a Greek tragedy,* The Oresteia, *by Aeschylus, and we decided that we would do the show in masks. We did an enormous amount of experimentation and what we began to realise was that the great potency of the masks; the audience actually projected their own feelings and their own emotions on to them. So it appeared that the masks changed at various times during the play when, of course, they didn't change at all. But your imagination was creating this change and filling in the think bubbles for the characters.*

And it occurred to me that that's exactly what great clowns do. Originally they would have done it by painting their faces white as a representation of a mask, and latterly when we got to silent comedy, they would have had a light make-up and this incredible stillness of face…a strong physical presence but a stillness of face. The great thing to me about Stan Laurel was that he was able to have this remarkable facial economy and yet, at the same time, put over this very appealing and put-upon guy.

Obviously, there was great craft in the way that Stan Laurel slowed down the action, and although this might seem like a simple idea when you see Laurel and Hardy do it, you are watching two great comic actors. And even if you slow things down, you still have to know when to move the action on again, which requires the most important gift that any comedian possesses: timing.

[Bruce Forsyth] *Their timing on screen is magical. The timing in good comedy, like* Only Fools and Horses, *or* The Two Ronnies, *or* Morecambe and Wise *has to be so exact. And some people in comedy today have no idea of timing. If they'd wait just that couple of seconds longer before doing the line, it would be so much better. Everything is a bit rushed, today. Laurel and Hardy, although they didn't have an audience, were able to ride the laugh they knew they would get, before coming in with the next line. And this is a great art. You can't teach people timing; they've either got it or they haven't. Laurel and Hardy were the best timers in the business.*

I try to ride a laugh, if there's a big enough laugh there, with just that look of frustration or even that look of pleasure. You get a big laugh, and you just ride on it, and you can't wait to get to the next line, but you just have to wait that few seconds before you come in with it.

But what happens when you don't have an audience with which to modulate the humour? When your comedy is being filmed in an empty studio. This problem can stump even the greatest comedians.

[Barry Cryer] *Morecambe and Wise never conquered films. Eric hated it because there was no audience to play off and he hated the waiting around and the silence of the film studio. And if you see their films, they're not good. The timing's not the same and they look stranded.*

Obviously Laurel and Hardy didn't have a studio audience to work off, either, but they used another device to help pace their films. When they had completed a picture, a cinema was chosen and the new film was slipped, unannounced, into the programme for a particular evening so that the people who came to watch acted as an unbiased preview audience.

One of the key functions of the preview was to gauge the length of the laughs, so that awkward pauses could be avoided at one extreme, and lines of dialogue didn't get swamped by laughter at the other. People from the studio would be dotted around the cinema scribbling notes in the darkness. Based on the audience's reaction, the movies were re-edited and certain scenes were even completely reshot. The film was then previewed a second time and the process repeated. There would then often be a third preview and re-edit before the film was deemed to be ready for release. This attention to detail was a key factor in making the Laurel and Hardy films work so well.

At these previews, the people from the studio were also in possession of hand-held counters, which they would click every time there was an appreciable laugh. These counts were then averaged to give a rough assessment of how well the movie was playing. However, there are two hazards in appraising a film in this way. Firstly, it may not be wise to trust the reaction of a particular audience on a particular night.

[Stan Laurel] *It's like being in vaudeville, every audience doesn't react in the same way. The first show can be a riot and the next show they don't know you're on the stage. So audiences differ, and their reactions differ. We'd do what you might call a milker routine and we'd take it to the preview. If, from the audience reaction, we felt they could stand more, we'd go back and add more to it. But sometimes our pictures were what you call 'over-milked.'*

This brings about an interesting point. Many people reading this book will never have seen Laurel and Hardy in a cinema, the setting for which their films were calibrated. Seeing them on television is a little like looking at wild animals in a zoo, and Stan himself, in later life, bemoaned this fact.

[Stan Laurel] *You watch any of the Laurel and Hardy pictures alone in a projection room, they look terrible. Doesn't seem to be a laugh in any of them. In the home, with just a couple or three people watching, they're wondering why the actors are standing still.*

Maybe Stan was stretching the point to make it more strongly, but like so many other people I have watched all the Laurel and Hardy films 'in the home' and have rarely had difficulty finding something to laugh at.

The other problem with appraising any film by its 'laugh count' is more subtle. The first ever episode of *Steptoe & Son* was made, not as a pilot for a series, but as one of several stand-alone episodes for a project called *The Comedy Playhouse*. It is interesting to listen to the reflections of the writers on how much comedy actually made it into the script.

[Galton & Simpson] *Some of the audience said the first episode was good,* The Comedy Playhouse *one, but everything after that deteriorated because it was played for laughs, or at least there were more laughs in it. Those are the purists. Obviously, if you see the first* Steptoe *now, Harry and Willy weren't playing it for laughs, they were playing it as a tragedy. They got a few laughs because these were written in…because we were comedy writers. But we were so pleased with the subject matter and the way it turned out, the fact that it didn't get many laughs didn't bother us at all. And it didn't matter to the actors because they came in on the strength of what they had read on the page. But once you start a comedy series, you start writing more comedy in. We didn't write the tragedy out if it, we just wrote more comedy in, but there was far more tragedy in the very first one.*

Obviously, the films of Laurel and Hardy are not often considered as tragedies, nor should they be, but there is a simple point in all this: if something is good, it's good, whether you laugh out loud right the way through, or not. If you are enjoying the film and enjoying being in the company of those characters, then metrics like 'laugh-count' or 'laugh-duration' become meaningless.

[Richard Wilson] *When directing a comedy for the stage, you realise, at the back of your head, that you've chosen to direct it because you think it's very funny, so you do feel a bit of a monster sending your actors out on the first preview, not knowing if there's going to be a laugh. But I don't laugh when I'm directing at all. A lot of directors laugh like drains; I think that's very dangerous. When you go out there on the first night, you don't know where your laughs will come from and the things that your fellow actors have laughed at in rehearsal, the audience usually don't find funny at all.*

At the early morning rushes, Stan Laurel reportedly used to laugh out loud at the material that had been shot the previous day. However, he never laughed during filming. He seemed to have a split personality in this regard. When he was shooting, it was all business and he was a complete professional. But when he then sat back and watched the results, he enjoyed them like any other viewer might.

With Laurel and Hardy, though, almost more remarkable than the 'laugh-count' is the 'smile-count.' All over the world, when those two characters appear, even if they are not doing anything, even if it is just in a still photograph, they have a remarkable ability to make people smile. The familiarity they have with the public creates a warmth and an almost instant appeal. It all comes back to character. So the next question to pose is: with this unique slower style now developed, and with the characters established, what sort of scrapes should these characters be placed in?

5. Story

Anyone who has written anything, from a documentary to an opera, will tell you about the importance of story. Stories are so much a part of how we make sense of the world that we scarcely notice them. We communicate through stories, we reconstruct the past with stories, we make sense of the present with stories, we fantasise about the future with stories, we entertain ourselves with stories, and we even dream in stories. Rarely will people talk about the story in a comedy they have seen – they will recall the funny moments – as they might after, say, a thriller or a drama, and yet story is the most important structural component in any comedy.

[Tony Robinson] *In* Blackadder, *we put a huge amount of work into the narrative. Narrative was all, as far as we were concerned. Narrative is the boat crossing the ocean that contains the jokes and the observations and the things that people laugh at. If you take the boat away, then the comedy just drowns.*

We tend not to notice stories in sitcoms unless they have failed in some way and, even then, most people are unaware of where the fault really lies.

[Stephen Merchant] *Often you will come back from the cinema with a friend who is not a particular aficionado of films or writing, and they'll say, 'That was a bit predictable.' And it seems to me that this is because the writers failed to disguise what was going to happen and you could second-guess it just from your knowledge of how stories unfold…like the boxer will get back in the ring, or whatever. In* The Office, *we know David Brent is going to get caught out in the end and embarrass himself, but we try to disguise the machinations that we have spent ages figuring out. John Cleese was brilliant at doing this in* Fawlty Towers *where he spent months working out a plot.*

There are occasions – thankfully very few – in the Laurel and Hardy short films, where a routine is allowed to run on too long and it becomes aimless and ultimately tiresome. One is where they spend too long getting changed for bed in a minuscule sleeper on a train in *Berth Marks*. Another is a sequence in *Be Big* where Ollie is trying to remove Stan's boots that he has mistakenly put on. It is interesting to reflect that, in each case, you are watching your heroes at the peak of their careers and yet, without the forward motion of narrative to breathe life into the situation, the sequences, although each is only a few minutes long, seem interminable.

Stories, particularly in a Laurel and Hardy two-reeler, don't have to be fiendishly intricate, but something reasonable has to happen, some challenge has to be put in front of the protagonists to prompt their actions. Challenges such as sweeping a chimney, fixing the leaks in a boat, putting up an aerial, breaking out of prison, escaping their wives for an evening at a speakeasy, adopting a child, smuggling a dog into a bed-sit, smuggling an ape into a bed-sit, buying ice cream, fleeing a vengeful murderer they have helped to convict, cleaning up Ollie's house after a wild party or simply delivering a piano…in one piece. Something has to be laid before the heroes to motivate their actions through the cause-and-effect intrigue of a story.

[Stan Laurel] *We turned tragedy into comedy. Many of our stories are shorts but could have been used, and have been used, in feature pictures as serious material. We took the other line, the humorous side of it. Sometimes there was a little pathos. I think this is good for a comic; it's necessary for a comic to have pathos.*

[Richard Wilson] *They had this great ability to just keep the storyline moving in a weirdly believable way.*

Most people would see the innocence of Laurel and Hardy as being a world away from cynical modern sitcoms, such as *The Office* or *Peep Show*. It might seem that the black and white, slightly cartoon world they inhabited is very far from our own, but from a story perspective, the motivations and conflicts are mined from the one seam.

[Stephen Merchant] *It seems to me that you could easily do a Laurel and Hardy film in which it is incredibly bleak and existential. Often the backdrop is poverty or depression or loveless marriages or uninspiring careers or aggressive neighbours. All those elements are there; it's just that they're not accentuated. Laurel and Hardy's behaviour overpowers them. We forget about the bleakness because we're too busy laughing at what they are doing. We were just a bit more willing to bring that bleakness to the forefront [in* The Office*] because people are willing to accept it a bit more, and it seems, then, to add a different note to things.*

[Andrew Sachs] *Really when you analyse it,* Fawlty Towers *is not funny at all; it's a tragedy. It's a tragedy of bad relationships and incompetence and everything that goes wrong in life. But it is angled in such a way that we see the absurd side of the tragedy and we can laugh at it. It's like a man slipping on a banana skin: it's funny because it's not us. That's the skill of it, it's a melodramatic piece, really.*

We probably all have a slightly patronising view of the cinema-going public of yesteryear – cap-wearing innocents guffawing jovially at unsophisticated, pratfalling silliness – but it should be remembered that these were extremely tough times, much tougher than today, and the people in the cinemas who came to see Laurel and Hardy were far from innocent. The situations that Laurel and Hardy found themselves in, reflected this reality. The adversity faced by the *Trailer Park Boys* is probably the nearest thing in sitcom, today.

[John Dunsworth] *Today, people see something like* Survivor *as a 'reality' TV show and it's so far from reality. But there's a reality in* Trailer Park Boys *in a funny way, and that's what people react to. They see people that they know. [Director] Mike [Clattenburg] really wants to have believable emotion in the characters. The audiences then see and experience situations that resonate with themselves. It's not a satire and it's not a parody. If you were to call it something, I guess you'd have to say it is a cautionary tale. It's really a bunch of losers who can't get their act together, just like Laurel and Hardy. Just like all of us…everybody. Look at*

George Bush – there's a clown. As soon as you say it can't happen, it happens next door.

The important point to make about stories in the Laurel and Hardy films is that they are not memorable or remarkable in their own right, and it is not for the story that people watch them. But if the story doesn't work, then the funny moments, which the viewers really do value, won't work either.

[Graham Linehan] *There's nothing intellectual about Laurel and Hardy but there is something special about the way these moments of cause and effect slapstick were arranged, where everything seems to be – as they say about all good writing – a fantastic mixture of the surprising and the inevitable.*

It is interesting to compare two Laurel and Hardy films on the basis of story. In *Going Bye Bye* (1934), their courtroom testimony helps to convict a notorious criminal played by Walter Long, who vows to escape and exact a violent revenge. In fear of this, our two heroes decide to leave town, but they need a companion to travel with them to share expenses, so they place an advertisement in the paper. However, the woman (played by Mae Busch) who answers this ad, happens to be a friend of the convict who has since escaped and arrived at her apartment seeking refuge.

When Stan and Ollie call to pick her up, thinking them to be the police, Mae Busch hides convict Long in a trunk and accidentally locks him in. Not knowing who's inside, Stan and Ollie then spend the rest of the film trying to free the very person they wish to flee. After being suffocated, blow-torched, and nearly drowned, Long finally escapes and administers his retribution on Stan and Ollie just seconds before the police arrive.

Compare this to Laurel and Hardy's second talking film, *Berth Marks* (1929). In this, the pair play a vaudeville act taking a train to Pottsville. On board, they inadvertently cause a fight which continues in their absence. They spend some time trying to find their bunk. Then they spend a much longer time trying to get changed for bed in a very cramped space. Just as they are about to settle down to sleep, the conductor announces that the next stop is Pottsville.

Of course, it is not reasonable to gauge how good or bad a film will be from a synopsis of the plot, but it may not surprise you to hear, if you haven't seen the two films, that *Berth Marks*, although it has some glorious moments, is leggy and confusing, whereas *Going Bye Bye* is one of their finest short films. Given that the same general working conditions existed in both cases, it is not unreasonable to conclude that it is the story that makes the difference, even in a tale as short as 20 minutes.

You can observe stories at work in everyday conversation. People don't aimlessly describe random events in their lives unless they align into some coherent point. This point may not be earth-shattering, but it will be useful or interesting on some level. You wouldn't describe your regular morning drive into work unless it was the drive during which you crashed the car, ran over a dog, got chased by a policeman, or drove into a large puddle in your open-topped Model-T and sank right up to your neck in water (*Perfect Day*, 1929). We have come to expect, as humans, a coherent direction to a story, so the action in even a two-reel comedy must go somewhere. There are many rules of thumb that govern the writing of these stories.

[Ardal O'Hanlon] *You always have to have a neat resolution; otherwise it won't work and people won't tune in next week. You start off with the situation and then have the craziness where everything gets turned upside down and then it all comes back together again. Anything can happen in the middle. As Geoffrey Perkins, the producer of* Father Ted, *used to say to me: 'Sitcoms are a beginning…muddle…and end.'*

It surprises many people, particularly first-time writers, that rules are hugely important to stories. Even the most fantastic flights of imagination are bound by the laws of the world in which they are created. However fantastical that world might be. It may be reasonable for a character to break into song in *My Fair Lady* or for a man to fly in *Superman*, but if someone were to suddenly take off in the former, or dance in the latter, most viewers would quickly lose interest. In the same way that the integrity of the characters must be served at all times, so too must the integrity of the environment they inhabit. In the sometimes zany world of comedy, it is easy to lose sight of this but no less damaging if you do.

[Graham Linehan] *There has to be a logic that holds the thing together. The furniture has got to be bolted down. It's something I thought about when I saw the second* Matrix *film: if anything can happen, then nothing matters. In comedy, if anything can happen, then nothing will be funny. People send me scripts, sometimes, where the characters behave exactly how the writer wants them to behave in order to service that one joke. A character will do a joke about what an idiot he is in one scene and in the next scene he'll be getting drunk and there'll be no explanation as to why there was this change in his character. You end up with a script that's really just a collection of words.*

Believing in the world you inhabit goes back again to believing in the character you are playing. An actor will not play a character well if he does not have sympathy and respect for that character. This applies to the David Brents, Basil Fawltys, Captain Mainwarings, and Alan Partridges of the comedy world. Although these people are foolish, you couldn't properly make fun of them, as an actor or writer, if you didn't feel for them in some way. You will never feel embarrassed for someone you dislike.

[Ardal O'Hanlon] *The more stupid it is, the more you have to play it for real. One of the reasons I loved playing Dougal was that it was pure escapism for me. It was like a retreat into childhood. You felt pure playing him; you felt that you weren't doing any harm to* *anybody. And I used to take it very seriously. You had to play it dead straight and really believe it. It wouldn't have worked if you'd played him like a stupid eejit; you had to inhabit that character, and be that person, who was as pure as the driven snow. I can't explain why I liked that, but I did.*

This respect and affection for the characters, and belief in the world they inhabited, is echoed in this quote by Oliver Hardy.

[Oliver Hardy] *Whenever I introduce Stan, it's always, 'I'd like you to meet my friend, Mr. Laurel,' and vice versa. These two people we created, they are very nice people. They never get anywhere because they are both so very dumb but they don't know that they're dumb. These two fellows have as much right to exist as anybody on earth, and they have just as much right to be called mister. Stan and Ollie are real people and they are good people. So, I don't feel bad that people connect me with a very dumb guy. In my opinion, he is also a very nice guy and there are a lot of him around.*

In the 1930 short, *Below Zero*, Laurel and Hardy are busking for pennies in the bitter cold when they have an altercation with a woman who ends up destroying their livelihood – a double-bass of Ollie's and a small portable organ of Stan's. This vandalism is a response to Stan throwing the woman's bucket of water into the street, so it seems a harsh retribution, but this is the cruel world in which Laurel and Hardy try to make their way. It really does look cold, they really do look tired and hungry, and Stan really does seem worried about his beloved instrument having seen what this formidable woman has done to Ollie's double bass. At the end of *Towed in a Hole* (1932), Stan runs to the wreckage of their car and boat which have been mangled together in a terrific crash, to see if he can retrieve his horn from the glove compartment. And he looks as pleased that this horn still works in *Towed in a Hole* as he looked inconsolable about his organ going under the wheels of a truck in *Below Zero*. The actors really believe in their characters, the situations they inhabit, and the stories they are enmeshed in and, as a result, so do the viewers.

[Graham Linehan] *In* Father Ted, *we wanted to show people that we were parodying sitcom and not really taking it seriously by originally having this silly little piece of music as the theme tune that sounded like the music from* The Good Life. *Our producer at the time said, 'Why do you want to make fun of your characters with this music? People will believe in these characters and will love them, so why do you want to make fun of them?' It was a very pivotal moment for me. I realised as he said those words that he was right and it made me think about everything in a very different way.*

This strange cosy affection can grow around even the most obtuse characters, if they are played with conviction. The familiarity that builds up with the characters leads to a warm feeling in the viewer every time he or she enters that comedy world.

[Nigel Planer] *We set out to do the most unattractive characters we could in* The Young Ones *and everyone ended up loving them. It's a mystery, although it often seemed to us that we four were like a comic mirror of the nuclear family, albeit a very dysfunctional one. Neil and Mike were the parents, and Rik and Vyvyan were the squabbling kids. Obviously one cannot take these kinds of analogies too far because they fall apart under the least scrutiny but I do feel that the unsophisticated, pre-verbal child is never far in a Laurel and Hardy film and this might go some way to explaining their universal appeal and also their decline when more grown up strictures were placed upon them, like having to fill out full-length stories.*

How, then, were the Laurel and Hardy stories written? The answer is: very differently from today. It started, each time, with a meeting between Stan Laurel, Hal Roach and a handful of writers. An idea would be thrown into the ring – often by Roach himself – and this would be brainstormed for a couple of hours. At this point, Roach would delegate one of the writers to do up a short treatment, which would outline the story without detailing specific gags.

Next, they would meet to discuss the gags, and the outline would be rewritten. This would then be presented to Stan, the director of the film, and a couple of the gag men. The gag men, as the name suggests, were the people who hovered around the set during shooting and helped to choreograph the workings of each specific routine. More discussions would ensue on the outline before this could be written up as a shooting script. However, although this three-to-six-page document was supposed to be the final plan of action, it was really only a starting point for the activities on set.

Deviations from the script were the norm, when shooting Laurel and Hardy films, not the exception. The story would depart from its original course in accordance with how the on-set team viewed the scenes that had already been choreographed and played. To facilitate this flexible approach, the films were shot in sequence. Even if the action was due to move between, say, a kitchen and a living room, they would shoot in one location, move to the other, and then go back in the first one, and so on. This meant that they were never hampered by having to bring the plot to a pre-filmed outcome. For a two-reel film, this process took about three weeks, at which time the films would be previewed, as described earlier. There was some overlap between films, but in the days of the early talkies, Laurel and Hardy were producing a comedy short at a rate of just under one per month.

Although this approach seems crazy by modern standards, it should be remembered that most of what Laurel and Hardy did was visual, not verbal, and this is obviously a lot harder to script in words than dialogue would be. And because the Roach Studios weren't too large, and since Laurel and Hardy were the studio's big stars, they could afford to be flexible in their working practices and take the time needed to get things right. It was time well spent.

The director of *Trailer Park Boys*, Mike Clattenburg, took a similar hands-on approach. Although the amount of unscripted material that made it into the final edit would be far less than was the case for Laurel and Hardy, he worked the situations until they seemed right to him.

[John Dunsworth] *Mike is always hoping that there's a mistake while we're rehearsing, so he can say: I want that. He takes a scene, and if it's not funny, he keeps shooting and he keeps directing and he keeps tweaking until he finds it funny. And if we're not delivering funny to him, he gets upset. Not with us, particularly, but he just becomes frustrated. He doesn't construct the laughs; he wants them to be there. Do I know where the laugh is going to be in my own lines? No, I do not.*

One of the things that facilitated Laurel and Hardy's ad-hoc approach was the fact that the Hal Roach Studios was like a family. The different facilities – production, writing, scripting, editing – were not compartmentalised, so everyone understood how the films were made. As a result, on-set improvisation wasn't the mess that it could have been in other hands. And, of course, many sitcom writers today brainstorm and improvise in the same way. They just tend to do so before going in front of the cameras.

[Stephen Merchant] *A lot of it is improvised into a Dictaphone, with each of us taking on different roles, so it's fairly organic.*

The approach of Stephen Merchant and Ricky Gervais brings up another similarity with the films of Laurel and Hardy in that more than one person was responsible for their writing. This has been true of many of the great sitcoms. So crediting Stan Laurel as being the creator of the Laurel and Hardy films is not accurate and something that Stan himself was always quick to correct.

[Stan Laurel] *No one man can make a picture. That's silly. I had some very fine boys who worked with me; we were all like a happy family. We would all have ideas. No one thought that one was any better than the other.*

Writing with someone else seems, from the outside, like a difficult thing to do and in, say, fiction writing it is almost unheard of. But in comedy, in particular for television, it is common and seems to benefit the script.

[Tony Robinson] *The reason that we got Ben Elton in [with Richard Curtis] is because we were so joke-light in the first series [of Blackadder]. But because they were both such incredibly good writers, within days they were mimicking each other's writing. So, after a few weeks, you'd get a really good knob gag and say to Ben, 'That's got to be you,' and he'd say, 'No, that was actually Richard.' And likewise, you'd get this really elaborate and gentle bit of plotting and you'd think that it had to be Richard and you'd find out it was Ben.*

[Stephen Merchant] *There's no obvious demarcation. Possibly when we first began, I was a bit more obsessed with structure but that isn't the case anymore and hasn't been for some time. It's much more fluid now and we're always in the room together. We spend a lot of time trying to hammer out plots and dynamics and hopefully once the characters are right and the scenes are right, then the jokes will almost write themselves.*

[Barry Cryer] *When John Junkin and I wrote for Morecambe and Wise, I was the 'sitter' and he was the 'walker.' It's an old cliché with two writers in a room that one would be scribbling or typing and the other would be walking about. John Junkin was a very good Eric Morecambe. He would twiddle his glasses, and you could hear Eric's voice in your head.*

Brilliant people break the rules like Johnny Speight and Eric Sykes who both wrote alone so you can't generalise, but I've always worked in partnership because if you have a mental block when you are writing on your own, you're in trouble. But if there are two or even three of you, you can start bouncing ideas around and something will happen.

This business of hammering out plots is something that writers often talk about but to which most viewers are oblivious. People remember funny moments from comedies, the jokes that *almost write themselves*, as Stephen Merchant terms them, but if the story is awry, the whole thing will fall apart. However, it is also important not to allow considerations of story to take over. A fine balance sometimes has to be struck between having a plot that does enough to motivate the actions of the characters without swamping the comedy completely.

[Graham Linehan] *The thing that we were trying to model the show on, in terms of story in the second and third series, was* Seinfeld, *which had a very strong story arc in each episode. But sometimes this could be to its detriment. Arthur [Mathews] might have been a little bit frustrated, on occasion, at how plotty the episodes were and I agree in the sense that in the third series, it took a bit more time to smell the roses.*

Sitcoms can become even more bogged down by elaborate plotting when there are inter-episode as well as in-episode story arcs. *The Office* is a notable and highly successful example of a series where threads – most notably the Dawn and Tim romance – develop over the course of the series. However, the desire to include series-spanning story arcs in *Trailer Park Boys* caused a lot of tension between the writers and the producers.

[John Dunsworth] *The people in [the TV channel] Showcase wanted the arc but, personally, I don't see the necessity. I think that if you can hold the audience's attention and thrill them – introduction, rising action, and climax – in the moment, and grab the audience for 22 minutes, then that's what is most important. But it's the way, now, if you want to write something and get funding, then you have to write it in the right terminology. And I think people get hamstrung when originality is really way more important.*

Within each episode of Trailer Park Boys, *there is a coherence. You'll notice that there are beautiful little denouements at the end of each episode. Clattenburg looks at every episode like a short film. I think the arc stuff drives him nuts. It's not important. What we're doing at a particular moment is important.*

With Laurel and Hardy, if anything, there was a slight tendency to under-plot. But apart from the occasionally tedious comic idea, in a 20-minute film, with protagonists who have a gift for spinning beautifully crafted routines out of really simple ideas, plot was rarely a problem. It became a problem, however, when they started to make feature-length films.

Financial pressure on the short-subject market was what eventually pushed Laurel and Hardy into making only feature films from 1935 onwards. But they made their first full-length film, *Pardon Us*, in 1930 for a very different reason.

[Stan Laurel] *We used to make the picture in whatever length it was good. In other words, we might start out to make a two-reeler but if it ran over to three, or three-and-a-half, or even four reels, and it previewed and we thought cutting anything would suffer the picture, we kept the length. So some of the films practically became featurettes.* Pardon Us *started as a two-reeler and ended up in four. After the preview there was nothing to cut so Roach said, 'Look, I'm tired of giving four reels of comedy at two-reel prices, so we'll add a couple more reels and make a feature out of it.'*

The flexibility to run longer would appeal to many writers who have to script to very precisely timed television slots, today. But there is a big difference between allowing a story to run on a little where appropriate and deliberately seeking to stretch an already completed film by 50 per cent. *Pardon Us* has some hilarious moments but it really doesn't work as a coherent film, and it presaged future problems in extending the Laurel and Hardy formula to stories of an hour or more.

Fundamental among these is a problem faced by all comics which is that, oddly, there seems to be an actual time-limit on how long people can laugh.

[Stephen Merchant] *There comes a point where after about 60 minutes, you can't have the same level of laughs and you've got to be telling a story. We had that problem with the* Extras *Christmas special, where Ricky couldn't be funny in the way that he had been previously because he needed to serve the story. So we had to do something with his character. We had to make him more villainous, let's say, for the purposes of our story. But this would then lead him* *to start losing sympathy with the audience, which would mean he wouldn't be as funny anymore because you couldn't laugh at him in the same way.*

Expanding successful sitcoms into movies became the fashion in the 1970s. Among others, the Steptoes, Dad's Army, Ronnie Barker and his cellmates from Porridge, and Morecambe and Wise found their ways onto the big screen, and although the results of these projects varied in quality, none came close to emulating the originals from which they spawned.

[Andrew Sachs] *I've never known it to work. I was in* Are You Being Served. *I wasn't in the show itself, but they asked me to be in the film, and it was terrible. I was the manager of the hotel which was bad casting because the one thing I shouldn't have played, after Manuel, was another Spaniard. It really wasn't funny at all.*

It is interesting to reflect on just how many comedy films (or how few) make you laugh all the way through.

[Stephen Merchant] *There are funny films but there are not many which work as a comedy and as a film. A spoof like* Airplane, *funny as it is, you could switch it off after ten minutes, you could switch it off after 40 minutes.*

Laughter, it seems, is like white-water rafting: in as much as it is exhilarating, it is also exhausting.

[Bruce Forsyth] *It's a tiring thing. When I've been with people that have made me laugh, at a dinner or having a drink – Tommy Cooper or Harry Secombe or Les Dawson or Frank Carson – they exhaust you because it's very funny and you laugh so much that you feel very tired and later on in the evening you wonder why you had to go to bed early.*

This is not, then, just a problem for comedy film-makers; in any scenario where people sit, listen and laugh, after a certain period of time attention seems to wander.

[Ardal O'Hanlon] *It's very hard to work in a longer format. In America, the main act would never perform for more than 40 minutes. My attention wanders after 40 minutes at a comedy gig, no* *matter who it is. I noticed this when I went to see Tommy Tiernan at the top of his game, in Vicar Street. He was playing to a devoted, reverent audience and yet after 45, 50 minutes, there was a real hiatus, where people start getting shifty in their seats and getting up to go to the toilet or to the bar. I also remember watching a very long Eddie Izzard gig when I was a big fan of his and being in genuine pain...I had a fierce headache.*

I used to have a support act and do an hour-and-five, or an hour-and-ten, and it was always the same: there was a huge hurdle to get across. Of course, it's easier if there is a story or some sort of a thread, where people can follow something and need to stay with you, but when you're just doing bits and pieces, the audience has every entitlement to switch off and zone out for a while. I've copped on. Last year when I toured, I did pretty much two 40-minute sets, and it worked so much better.

Forty to 50 minutes seems to be the limit, after which comedy needs to develop into something different or simply take a break. Something else needs to emerge as gag upon gag ceases to work. Episodes of a sitcom, running for 25 to 30 minutes, or Laurel and Hardy shorts, fit well within this threshold but feature films exceed it. So how do you make comedy work in this longer format?

[Stephen Merchant] *In the early Marx Brothers films, they essentially run around being mad for 65 minutes and it's very funny but kind of exhausting. You're enjoying it, but there's no real story there. And then Irving Thalberg [at MGM] said we could halve the laughs and get three times as much at the box office by introducing people who aren't comedy characters, who are maybe in love but are being kept apart for some reason, and then the Marx Brother's tomfoolery is serving that story. So now you're watching the Marx Brother's fun but the story is when these young lovers get together. Now there's a reason why the Marx Brothers are running around like lunatics.*

Thalberg got the Marx Brothers to thread a strong story structure through their films, added a main plot with straight actors for them to work off, and included noncomic musical numbers. Which is exactly what Laurel and Hardy had done a couple of years earlier.

Feature films were much more lucrative for the studio than shorts, and there was an inexorable trend in cinemas towards double-feature programmes which would eventually extinguish the market for two- and three-reelers entirely. Laurel and Hardy made a second feature film, *Pack Up Your Troubles* (1932), which played to mixed reviews before, under pressure from Hal Roach, they accepted the idea in *Fra Diavolo* (1933) of doing what the Marx Brothers would come to do under Thalberg and essentially made themselves the sub-plot of their own movie. *Fra Diavolo* was the first of their comic operas, and it was also the longest film they ever made, running for 90 minutes.

Although *Fra Diavolo* works quite well, there is an absurdity in introducing irrelevant, extraneous material just to make the Laurel and Hardy comedy work better in features when it was working just fine in shorts. People come to a Laurel and Hardy film to see Laurel and Hardy, not musical routines, however lavishly choreographed or beautifully sung. In other films, such as *Bonnie Scotland*, the main plot they sub off, although song-less, is pointless. Also, there is little connection between the nominal main plot and Laurel and Hardy's comic interludes. They may counterpoint each other, but the comic relief is as much a *relief* from having to sit through the main story as it is joy in seeing the real heroes of the piece.

A few of their feature films did have Laurel and Hardy front and central with no padding, and did manage to work, most notably *Sons of the Desert* (1933), which is pretty near seamless. Another is *Way Out West* (1936). It should be noted, though, that these two films run for only just over an hour and nothing released in the cinema today is even nearly that short. Many fans of Laurel and Hardy will also be aware that there *are* two musical numbers in *Way Out West* – 'At the Ball, That's All' and 'Trail of the

Lonesome Pine' – but both are performed by Stan and Ollie themselves and are among most people's favourite Laurel and Hardy moments.

Generally, though, the Laurel and Hardy feature films were always fighting against themselves. Either they abdicated responsibility for the main plot and risked boring the audience with what was essentially filler, or they tried to carry everything on their own shoulders and risked stretching their beautifully crafted silliness to its limits of lightness.

As Hal Roach came under increasing pressure to make feature films, friction started to grow between the studio head and his biggest stars. A longer film, as well as being much harder to make, was necessarily a bigger gamble as Roach could only produce maybe two each year. This led him to take a greater role in production, in particular in the crafting of stories. In this area, Roach and Laurel quarrelled frequently.

In later interviews, Roach was scathing about Stan Laurel's abilities in regard to story. Whether these criticisms are justified or not, a rift formed between Stan Laurel and his employer which would widen in the latter half of the decade and eventually lead to Laurel and Hardy leaving Hal Roach in 1940.

Up until the mid-1930s, the pair continued to make short films but when they had shot the last of these, *Thicker Than Water* (1935), it is sad to acknowledge that their greatest days were behind them. They moved to 20th Century Fox where they had full-time writers working for them but the films they made there, and later at MGM, were dire. Principal among the reasons for this was the fact that the writers didn't take time to understand the characters and although the films were heavily plotted, it should be clear by now that if you don't know your characters, you will never write a good story in which to place them.

6. Actions & Reactions

Very often it is the reaction to a funny moment that makes it really funny. It's like a punctuation mark, a point of inflection that gives the humour its beat. The Laurel and Hardy films were a veritable study in reactions; each comic's humour being made funnier by the other.

[Graham Linehan] *With every single joke in Laurel and Hardy, you get three for the price of one. You usually get Ollie's reaction, and then you get Stan's reaction, and then you get Ollie's reaction to Stan's reaction…and often they will go one further and cut back to Stan. And these three or four reactions each get a laugh.*

There is something fundamental about the idea of reactions in comedy. In many ways, comedy is like the riddle of the tree falling in the forest – if the moment isn't witnessed, can it be said to have been funny? How often have you experienced something in exasperation or disillusionment or disbelief, to later laugh about it when relating the incident to friends?

[Galton & Simpson] *You have to have somebody to bounce off. When you have two, you can really explore the characters.*

[Stephen Merchant] *The dynamic in* Extras, *between Ricky [Gervais] and Ashley [Jensen] was explicitly a Laurel and Hardy. We sat down and said let's do an idiot and another idiot, except we'll just make one of them a woman. In fact* Extras *is almost entirely Laurel and Hardy, just differently apportioned: Me and Ricky, Me and Shaun [Williamson], Ricky and Ashley, Me and Ashley. Whatever it is, it's really just a Laurel and Hardy set-up.*

Sometimes something that wasn't even particularly funny can be made funny by the reaction alone. And in extreme cases, a reaction is not even required; the absence of a reaction can say it all.

[Barry Cryer] *Humphrey Lyttelton could get a laugh out of silence. You could almost see him when you were listening to the radio* *at home. One of us would have sung a song or something [on* Sorry I Haven't a Clue*] and there would be a bit of applause and then nothing would happen for a few seconds and the audience would laugh. The people there could see him, obviously, but in a way at home you could get it, as well…that Humph was just thinking, 'Oh, God, let's move on to the next thing,' but he would say this with a silence.*

With Laurel and Hardy there were more than just the reactions to each other. There were the interactions with the people they brushed up against in what is usually a very hostile world. These other characters were a hugely important part of what made Laurel and Hardy work. They had to act, for the viewer, as a soundboard for Stan and Ollie's daftness, and do so in a believable way.

[Stephen Merchant] *It has to feel real. They have to be credible people because reacting to stuff is very hard to do. You need someone to witness the comic behaviour of Stan and Ollie, as this makes it funnier. It was exactly the same with us. It was important that there were people to bump up against, in particular for David Brent. It might be his boss or some people who come in to interview him, or someone whom he is in competition with…but they have to do it very well because, as we all know, it's so hard to do the straight-man's job.*

The supporting players were very important in making the Laurel and Hardy comedy work, and one of the few benefits of being forced into making feature films was that the supporting players had time to become more real as characters. This allowed for a greater intricacy in the interplay between the supporting cast and Stan and Ollie. A scene from *Sons of the Desert* – the ultimate fool-the-wives caper – illustrates this beautifully. Stan and Ollie have pledged to go to a convention in Chicago but have not yet asked their wives. When they get home, Stan is locked out of his house so he waits with his next-door neighbours, the Hardys, until his wife returns.

The ensuing scene is a beautiful plait of interactions: Ollie tactfully trying to work around his wife; Stan trying to understand the subtext and not exasperate the fearful Mrs Hardy; Ollie giving various dirty looks to Stan; Stan putting his foot in it anyway; Mrs Hardy telling her husband what's what; Stan asking Ollie if he's going to stand for such a telling off when Mrs Hardy leaves the room; Ollie incited to rebellion by Stan's baiting until his wife returns, crockery in hand. The scene only works because of the comic aplomb of Mae Busch, sparking off the two leads. The same is true of James Finlayson in *Our Relations* (1936), where he gives surely his most subtle and funny performance, pitted against not just Stan and Ollie but also their identical twin brothers, Bert and Alf.

With Laurel and Hardy, as with *The Office*, there was yet another level of interaction for the comedy, namely that between the actors and the viewer. In *The Office*, it is the conceit that the whole thing is being filmed as part of a fly-on-the-wall documentary that allows the fourth wall to be broken. The inspiration for this came from Laurel and Hardy where Ollie is allowed to communicate with us as we watch.

[Stephen Merchant] *We used to say to the actors on set, 'Give us an Oliver Hardy.' We'd say to Martin Freeman, 'We just need an Ollie there,' which would be short-hand for look at the camera and essentially roll your eyes as if to say, 'Have you just witnessed that?' And we had very specific directions, which were that you don't move your head, just your eyes, and let them register the camera and then flick back to the action. They were all carefully put in.*

This checking in with the audience makes the action funnier and not only is it a way of reacting to something that has just happened but also of building anticipation of what is to come.

[Stephen Merchant] *There's one Laurel and Hardy film where they're in the sawmill* [Busy Bodies] *and Ollie has a brush stuck to his chin, and he decides to let Stan shave him [with a wood plane], and he glances at the camera as if to say, 'We know this is an absurd* *idea but have you got a better suggestion?' It's that constant relationship with the viewer that makes the situation funny.*

And, as with everything else in Laurel and Hardy, these reactions happened slowly.

[Nigel Planer] *For me, the pace was not so frenetic…reaction shot…reaction shot…reaction shot.*

[Richard Wilson] *All those reactions…it's all thought, isn't it? It's all changing the thinking.*

Both Stan Laurel and Oliver Hardy had the ability to be the comedian and the straight man. This allowed a rich, voiceless interplay on even the simplest comic moments. And they were not only masters of reacting to each other, or to the people around them, but also to the inanimate objects that assailed them with improbable frequency.

[Graham Linehan] *Everything in Laurel and Hardy, through sound effects, looks incredibly painful. If a brick falls on Ollie's head, you really feel it…partly, obviously, owing to Ollie's acting ability. He always looks like he's really unnerved by anything that happens to him.*

[Nigel Planer] *I think, from what I've worked on, Rik [Mayall] and Adrian [Edmondson] were like Laurel and Hardy in the very meticulous way they smashed everything up.*

What makes all these reactions work is the rhythm and pace of the pair's delivery. Timing of this sort is the great skill of any comic actor, but it is not just the rhythm of delivery that is crucial but the rhythm of the material in the script they are working from. The actors and the script are two sides of the same coin, and the comedy won't succeed if either fails. Even though the comedy of Laurel and Hardy was largely visual rather than verbal, and even though much of it was worked out on the set, the same care had to be taken in planning, sequencing, and pacing the events as did in acting them out. This pacing of the script, be it verbal or visual, is vital if the actors are to stand any chance of bringing the characters to life.

[Galton & Simpson] *If you were writing for Sid [James], you had to take as much trouble as if you were writing for Hancock. The straight lines were just as important as the tagline. You didn't want to lose the audience halfway towards the punchline, so the feed lines had to be as well written. We used to avoid lines like 'And then what happened, Tony?'; 'Oh really? And what are you doing now, Tony?'*

There is a certain un-analysable pace to well-written comedy but in truth, this pacing is present in all forms of writing.

[Galton & Simpson] *Rhythm is just as important in prose and just as evident with great writers in the way they structure their lines. Graham Greene is an example of near-perfect structure. In his own way, Dickens is the same. And Mark Twain...who is a little bit more verbose, but his writing is all beautifully structured. This is very important in all writing, not just dialogue that's going to be said by actors.*

Some writers work with the actors in achieving this, others are more prescriptive in how they want things to be done but either way, in all great comedy, there is a perfect match between the script and the actors. It is true of all the very best sitcoms that you could never imagine anyone else playing the lead role. It is not surprising, for example, that when David Renwick wrote *One Foot in the Grave*, he always had Richard Wilson in mind for the part of Victor Meldrew. We think of comedians and comic actors when we talk of timing but there must also be timing in the script if the comedy is to work.

[Richard Wilson] *Writing was a very agonising process for David [Renwick]. He slaved over those scripts, so by the time you got them, they were pretty hot...damn near perfect. His rhythms were wonderful. He knew what he was doing, so you had to hit the right pacing and the right rhythm.*

[Tony Robinson] *All great comedy is about rhythm as much as anything else and comedians are people who work in rhythm and trade in rhythm. And that can be a beat within the dialogue or* *within the joke itself. So, deep in the heart of every good comedian, rhythm is pounding away like a heartbeat. For that reason, I wouldn't be surprised if you found that a lot of good comedians had an affinity with music.*

A simple instance from a single Laurel and Hardy film might help to illustrate the care with which they crafted the reactions to each single comic moment. In the 1930 short, *Blotto*, there is a scene where Stan is going out to meet Ollie although he has told his wife that he has been called away on 'important business.' Just as he is about to leave, his wife, played by Anita Garvin, asks Stan if he has forgotten something and, after pondering this for a moment, Stan returns and gives her a kiss on the cheek. Then, when he makes to leave a second time, he walks the wrong side of the front door and straight into the wall. This is a simple visual gag and it was done, with subtle variation, in a number of films. But it is interesting to look more closely at how the comic moment is punctuated by reactions.

First, there is the painfully loud bang as Stan hits the wall (he is out of sight behind the door). Second, his hat is seen to fly into shot from the impact and land at Anita Garvin's feet. Third, there is a phonograph on the near side of the door, with its lid up, and at the point of impact, the lid crashes heavily down. Fourth, two small pictures fall from their mounts on the wall above the phonograph. Fifth, there is the reaction of Garvin – a restrained flinch and an expression that reads, 'Oh for heaven's sake!' And finally, there is the reaction of Stan himself, who reappears, slowly rubbing his nose and mouth in seeming genuine pain. And even for the next shot, from outside the house, Stan is still smarting from the impact. The point is that the viewer will remember only the gag – Stan walking into a wall – and none of these small details will be memorable in their own right, but they are all carefully included to accentuate the comic moment like a cymbal crash.

The rhythm in Laurel and Hardy is not just verbal but visual, and few television sitcoms of the modern age have employed physical and visual humour to any large degree. One exception is *Fawlty Towers*, in particular in the interplay between Basil and Manuel, for which an apprenticeship in taking falls was required.

[Andrew Sachs] *I was playing the lead in* No Sex Please, We're British, *which was started by Michael Crawford and he put a lot of acrobatic stuff into the part. I played that, with all the Michael Crawford gags, for about a year, so I was used to throwing myself about. In* Fawlty Towers, *it was the writers who wrote the physical side into the role but I happened to be the right person for that part. Then I could elaborate and come up with ideas, some of which were accepted and developed. The whole thing grew in the rehearsal period.*

One of the things that helped the timing and rhythm of the Laurel and Hardy films was freshness. Stan Laurel felt that lightness was vital to comedy, and this would be lost by over-rehearsing. So although everything was carefully planned, it was captured as soon as it could be.

[Stan Laurel] *We'd work out a script and get to shooting it as quick as we could. I don't believe in sitting for weeks and months on a picture…comedy especially. It can't be done, particularly this type of comedy.*

This belief, coupled with the professionalism of both men and the natural physical rapport between them, meant that most scenes were shot once and once only.

[Stephen Merchant] *Ricky is very good, that way. He always wants to get the camera running, to catch the alchemy which dissipates quickly when you over-rehearse something.*

Of course, this kind of process has to be tight, since freshness can soon turn to looseness, and freedom to anarchy.

[Tony Robinson] *On* Blackadder, *it was very collective. It wasn't hierarchical at all. But when you've got 36 hours to go to* *taping the show and we were still all talking, then obviously the producer had to come in and make some executive decisions. But up till that moment, we were all involved in developing the characters, the language, and the scenes.*

Laurel and Hardy were able to shoot most of their routines in a single take. This, however, only worked because of the professionalism of the two actors. This is echoed by one of the greatest on-the-spot improvisers, and one of the greatest professionals, on British television, Bruce Forsyth.

[Bruce Forsyth] *I always like the unknown to happen. If the unknown happens, I look at that as a challenge: how can I get out of it? If something has gone wrong, I'm glad it's gone wrong. It gives me something to think about. And I can well imagine when Laurel and Hardy had a basic synopsis of what they were going to do, many things could come along…the director, the producer, one of the stage crew or the camera crew would say, 'Oh it would be funny if…'. I should imagine that a lot of it was off-the-cuff and things were added to the situation, and I'd say that was half the fun of it. They must have been wonderful days of comedy.*

In 2003, Bruce Forsyth took the reins in the BBC's flagship panel show *Have I Got News For You* and famously brought the house down. But he is quick to acknowledge that his ability to improvise, build a rapport with the audience, and ride the humour of what was going on around him was greatly helped by the planning and professionalism of the show's writers.

[Bruce Forsyth] *I was very lucky, there, because they wrote the show around me. The show has a wonderful team of comedy writers and producers. When I went along to have the first read-through, I read this bit about 'Play Your Iraqi Cards Right' and I started to laugh and said 'You're not going to really do this? Are you just having a laugh with me this afternoon?' And they said, 'No, we want you to do it that way.'*

Laurel and Hardy's ability to shoot most scenes without a rehearsal or a re-take contributed to one money-making innovation adopted by Hal Roach in the early 1930s. In nine of their short films and their first feature, *Pardon Us*, they reshot the talking scenes in Spanish, French, German and Italian – although not all films in all languages – by reading the words phonetically from cue-cards. And although the process was both time-consuming and expensive – involving interpreters, language coaches and replacement supporting actors – it paid large dividends among the peoples of Europe, South America, and North Africa, who could now hear the friends they had made during the silent era, speaking to them in their own language. And it is among the audiences, English-speaking or otherwise, that yet another layer of reactions is at work.

As described in the last chapter, the Laurel and Hardy comedies were previewed and re-edited so that the pacing of the gags would match the laughter of a full cinema. However, this effect would be lost on television, where the audience drops in size from two or three hundred to just two or three. In the early days of television in the 1950s, it was felt that this would rob the comedy of a crucial dynamic and might make it play less funny.

[Galton & Simpson] *There's nothing more flat than going to an empty cinema or an empty theatre and watching a comedy. Producers at the time took the view that if there was no audience, then people sitting at home would themselves not laugh, and probably find it less funny. They felt that for a comedy, people like to have that backup to their feelings; if the people in the studio are laughing, then they can laugh. And I think there is probably an element of truth in that.*

So was born one of the strangest conceits in television: the studio audience. It is an odd thing when you think about it: you watch a comedy on television, that is itself being watched by an audience, who you cannot see, and the actors pretend they cannot see either, but both you and the actors can hear. The scenario is not without its difficulties.

[Richard Wilson] *I think it was John Thaw who said that sitcom is the hardest job for an actor because you've got to obey the camera and the shooting script but you have an audience there telling* *you not to. So you're juggling the two all the time. The great debate is: do you have an audience or not? I always really liked the audience, ultimately. I always felt that we got a lift from it and I think it helped a bit.*

There is a simplified view that studio audiences are old-fashioned and a new wave of slicker comedy – *The Office*, *Peep Show*, *The Royal Family* – has done away with them. However this view doesn't really hold water since the most cynical panel shows – *Have I Got News For You* among them – thrive, in part, on the energy of the studio audience and as far back as the 1970s and early 1980s, shows like *M*A*S*H* and *The Comic Strip Presents* didn't use them at all.

[Graham Linehan] *I think studio audience sitcoms are a style of sitcom, rather than something that's necessarily old-fashioned. If you have a sitcom with a bigger, more slapsticky feel, like say* The Young Ones *or* Blackadder *or* Father Ted, *then I think it's nice to have an audience there watching it with you.* The Office, *on the other hand, is unimaginable with a studio audience because of its style. I found the idea that studio audiences are dead an annoying point of view because it just seems to be based on fashion and fashion is fatal for comedy and also, really, for rock music. They're two genres where you really need to ignore fashion.*

The relationship between a sitcom and a studio audience, however, is a two-way thing. Insofar as certain comedy favours a studio audience, so the presence of a studio audience will pull the comedy in a certain direction.

[Galton & Simpson] *In the early days, all comedy shows featured comedians who reacted to audiences. They weren't actors, and they weren't used to going out and doing their thing regardless of the audience. But as you gradually start to write the situation for actors, as we did, you get a totally different performance. If* Steptoe *was being done today, I think there's no doubt that it would be done without a studio audience and therefore would develop differently. If you've got a studio audience and they don't laugh, it's telling you* *something. Without a studio audience, it throws a whole different light on the thing, and it will go in a different direction.*

The comedy must be amenable to a studio audience but when it is, the atmosphere created can really energise the show.

[Graham Linehan] *David Walliams once described it to me as a kind of fairy dust that you get with a studio audience. The only problem is that you spend your entire life trying to explain to people that it's not canned.*

[Ardal O'Hanlon] *It is cosy. It's very intimate and you really do feel that you own the space, particularly by the time you get to a second or third series of something. It's like your home from home. The audience are really in on it and are usually fans of the show. You often hear cynical commentators questioning the authenticity of the laughter; very rarely, in my experience, has a laughter track been used or canned laughter as it's known. Generally, if anything, even in poor sitcoms – God knows, I've worked on a few of those – the audience are laughing uproariously. They are fans of the show and they're there because they want to be there, or [laughing] because they've nothing else to do. If anything, what happens is you have to take some of the laughter away, so this suggestion of canned laughter is rubbish. I've seen it done on sketch shows where the sketches are played into an audience, so I guess that's canned in a way but it's still real laughter by real people.*

The studio audience is there to cajole the viewers at home into laughing, but it can happen that the laughter, owing to in-studio conviviality or the giddiness of a particular audience, can go over the top.

[Richard Wilson] *David Renwick wrote a solo episode for me in* One Foot in the Grave, *and there was a bit where Victor was lying on the couch doing a crossword with a leaking biro, and we actually had to stop recording because the audience wouldn't stop laughing.*

Again, it is strange to reflect that many people reading this book will not have seen Laurel and Hardy whilst sitting in a large group, so this dynamic – the studio-audience effect

– will never have been experienced. However, despite Stan Laurel's misgivings over the unsuitability of the original edit of the films for television, it hasn't stopped several subsequent generations from loving these films. Maybe this arises from the fact that most people who like Laurel and Hardy have grown up with them and accepted a rhythm and pace, as well as a lack of colour, that modern audiences might find jarring if they hadn't been weaned in the same way. But this raises another remarkable aspect of the Laurel and Hardy films: the way they were funny across the generations.

Certainly people come to appreciate comedy differently as they get older but the really best stuff seems to be able to straddle the generations. Most of the comedies I loved as a child – *Laurel and Hardy*, *Some Mothers Do Ave Em*, *The Young Ones*, *Only Fools and Horses*, *Porridge*, *Steptoe & Son* – I still love today. Although certain jokes might have gone over my head at the time, there was something in the characters and the rhythm of the delivery that was funny to me then and which is still funny to me now.

One of the things that might have helped Stan Laurel in this regard is the fact that he honed his comic instincts in vaudeville, where the audience was of a mixed age. Bruce Forsyth had a similar apprenticeship.

[Bruce Forsyth] *Nearly all my shows have been to a family audience and I feel lucky because if you were a comic today starting around the clubs, you'd get used to working to a club audience, which is much more abrasive. My mother and father used to take me to see variety shows when I was only about 11 or 12 and all around you'd see families. This is very unlike today, where in a television audience there's hardly any children.*

Playing to a variety audience may have helped Stan Laurel to see past the contemporary references of the time and the wording of specific jokes to something more universal in the same way that Bruce Forsyth was able to do many years later.

[Bruce Forsyth] *The audience on* Have I Got News For You, *although they were an audience that likes satire and put-down humour about politicians and so on, in five minutes after I'd been on, they were just like a gameshow audience. They were no different from a variety audience at a light entertainment show.*

The thing that probably most served the actions and reactions between Laurel and Hardy was that single mysterious quality called rapport, the basic harmony that oils conversations between close friends and makes certain situations feel unusually fluid and relaxed. On-screen, between Laurel and Hardy, there was a chemistry, both physical and psychological, that made them a pleasure to be with. And although it shouldn't really matter, most fans of Laurel and Hardy will be curious to know how they got on when the cameras stopped rolling.

The truth is they got on exceptionally well and yet almost never socialised or saw one another between films.

[Stan Laurel] *At the studio, we'd get through with a picture and I probably wouldn't see him again until we made the next one. He liked to golf, I liked to go fishing. My interest was in the pictures, he had no interest whatsoever in writing or producing. He said himself that he preferred to keep out of it. Just having to do it was enough, that was all that he wanted. Oh, he enjoyed it and I was glad to see him when he came back…it was a reunion sort of thing* [laughs].

There doesn't seem to be a single reported disagreement between the pair. No one who knew them or worked with them ever alluded to friction, frustration, or disharmony of any sort during the 30 years that Laurel and Hardy were partners. As already mentioned, Oliver Hardy had no creative ambitions which may well have contributed to the equanimity of his working relationship with Stan.

[Oliver Hardy] *Not that I didn't appreciate a good gag, mind you. I like to get a good reaction just the way any comedian does but I have never really worked hard in the creative department. After all, just doing the gags is hard enough work, especially if you've taken as* *many falls and been dumped in as many mudholes as I have. I think I've earned my money.*

[Barry Cryer] *It's the classic pattern with double-acts I've noticed through the years: there's the laid-back one and the worrier. It was very much true with Morecambe and Wise. Ernie was off on his boat, saying, 'Oh, speak to Eric about that,' while Eric was the script man and he was the worrier.*

Laurel and Hardy did get to know each other a lot better, however, in the late forties when they made the first of three tours of Britain. They had ended their demoralising association with the big studios in 1945 and had subsequently become largely forgotten by Hollywood. But in 1947 they travelled to Britain for what was supposed to be a six-week theatre tour and were once again overwhelmed – as they had been when they visited in 1932 – by the, at times, dangerously large and enthusiastic crowds that came out to hail them. This tour ended up taking in venues in several northern European countries and lasted for 11 months. They toured again in 1952 and 1953, and one of the contributors to this book managed to catch them during their last performances before ill-health forced Oliver Hardy back to America.

[Barry Cryer] *I saw them live in the Empire Theatre in the fifties and, in a way, although it was wonderful to see them, it wasn't a great show. There were effects that they couldn't reproduce live as well as they could on film and they were both older men and not very well at the time but they got a standing ovation because it was a personal appearance; it was very touching. This was pre-Beatles and yet people were queuing around the block to see them and Ollie stood there with tears streaming down his face. They probably thought after their great careers that they were sort of has-beens and when they came to Europe I don't think they quite expected the reaction they got – the sheer love of the audiences. They were knocked out by it.*

In this period, Laurel and Hardy obviously spent a lot of time together and once again there are no accounts of any discord between the two men.

You often hear stories of partnerships, in all artistic fields, that are fuelled by jealousy and creative competitiveness, so it would be wrong to state that Laurel and Hardy's off-screen civility was a necessary foundation for their on-screen actions, reactions, and interactions. But it did at least keep them together long enough to make a great many great films.

7. Supporting Roles

For the Laurel and Hardy films to work, the characters had to inhabit a believable world. Although Stan and Ollie were the principal sources of comedy within this world, the people they brushed up against had to be as in-tune with the comedy as they were.

As any book on creative writing will tell you, all good stories need conflict, and Laurel and Hardy met conflict around every street corner. They were always confronted by formidable supporting characters in their little tales of woe, be they judges, policemen, drill sergeants, sheriffs, bailiffs, wives, landlords, butlers, burglars, murderers, women across the hall, husbands of women across the hall, dogs, goats, apes, lions, ice-cream vendors, fathers-in-law, blackmailing harpies, and even ghosts. But one crucial factor is that although the masks changed, the players remained largely the same.

[Ardal O'Hanlon] *One of the very striking things about Laurel and Hardy is the strength of the supporting players; they were a kind of supergroup of comedy.*

As explained earlier, Laurel and Hardy emerged from a concept called the 'Comedy All-Stars' and although they very soon became named stars in their own right, other members of the group continued to appear on a regular basis in their films. These included James Finlayson (the bushy-moustached, eyebrow-raising, Scot), Mae Busch (the at times shrewish, at times charming, female lead), Charlie Hall (the diminutive, slow-burning owner of the shop next door in *Tit for Tat*, 1934), Billy Gilbert, Anita Garvin, Walter Long, Arthur Housman, Edgar Kennedy, Vivien Oakland and Tiny Sandford. The fact that these people appeared and reappeared helped to maintain the integrity of the Laurel and Hardy world.

In the years that Laurel and Hardy made their films at the Hal Roach Studios, many different supporting players were used but in any one film, there were only a few additional characters so as not to dilute or convolute the comedy.

[Ardal O'Hanlon] *If there are too many extraneous characters, it won't work because the whole thing about sitcom is familiarity. You really want to be with those people. The plot and the characters don't have to be too elaborate, you just need to have these people in a very normal everyday situation and move it along gently.*

Aside from strong characters like James Finlayson who was funny in his own right, the integrity and realism with which the support players acted their roles was crucial in making the situations funny.

[Tony Robinson] *One of the big secrets of comedy is good casting.*

[Stephen Merchant] *We auditioned all the supporting characters endlessly. Everyone who came in with a significant role to play, we auditioned. And we always had very specific types of people in mind.*

This is true in all of the great sitcoms, and yet it is something that doesn't draw attention to itself. These supporting actors need to have a keen sense of the comedy happening around them, without themselves necessarily being comedians.

[Galton & Simpson] *When we used to get comedians, they used to ham it up. We wanted to get away from these funny, eye-rolling, blokes pulling funny faces, and get straight actors playing it right down the middle, playing it as if they were playing Hamlet. Colin Gordon and Dudley Foster and people like that were beautiful to play against. Colin Gordon used to always play doctors and solicitors for us and he was dead straight but completely aware of the humour; that's the key. You get those blokes, they're gold dust.*

There are many examples of support players of this ilk in the films of Laurel and Hardy. An interesting case in point is Richard Cramer. Appearing in only four films, Cramer is known to most Laurel and Hardy fans as the very formidable judge in *Scram* (1932), the cruel foster parent in *Pack Up Your Troubles* (1932), and the gun-toting villain, Nick Grainger, in *Saps at Sea* (1939). Cramer doesn't utter a single comic line in any of these films; he is simply there as a foil, and a very menacing foil at that. But for Cramer to work in a Laurel and Hardy film, he must be in tune with the timing and pace of the comic leads. Cramer is probably the straightest of straight men in the world of Laurel and Hardy, but his very convincing performances only work because of the actor's understanding of the comedy happening around him.

This idea of casting actors with a sense of comedy does not have to be restricted to the supporting players, either. The leads in *One Foot in the Grave* are a good example.

[Richard Wilson] *Annette [Crosbie] had never done sitcom, and I think she was slightly more terrified than I was, in the beginning. And although I had done one, I had never had my name above the titles, as it were. We were actors, not comedians. When I'm asked about it, I always say the success of* One Foot in the Grave *was down to David Renwick and his great writing. And David Renwick, when he's asked, says it was down to us having a sense of comedy.*

David Renwick applied his insight in this respect to casting the supporting characters as well, and it created a rich world in which Victor Meldrew could pitch his battles. *One Foot in the Grave* boasts more characters who are funny in their own right, and who get laughs, than most sitcoms.

[Richard Wilson] *Many people said to me that Mrs Warboys, played by Jean Mantle, was their favourite character in the show.*

For the stars of the show, as well as the supporting players, it again comes back to serving the character and allowing the humour to arise out of the situation.

[Andrew Sachs] *I consider myself a character actor, really. If there is something funny or humorous in a character, then I'll try and bring it out. It's in my nature to do that, but I don't like superimposing comedy when there really isn't any there.*

For Laurel and Hardy to be funny, it was important to have a supporting cast who witnessed their silliness and reacted in a realistic way. Because many of the same actors were used again and again – James Finlayson, Charlie Hall, and Mae Busch each appeared in dozens of Laurel and Hardy pictures – there was a tightness and a consistency to the on-set team. Camaraderie among the crew has been a powerful creative force for some sitcoms.

[Tony Robinson] *On* Blackadder, *they would give us the script on the Monday, and we'd do the read-through and fall about laughing. By the time they came back on the Friday, we'd actually invented new characters and new endings to the episode. We'd gone so far down that line that they felt they no longer had possession of it and that was where the tensions arose.*

[Nigel Planer] *The comic strip films were good ongoing work. It was nice to be able to work with the same gang of people.*

[Stephen Merchant] *There's some improvisation, but generally we stick to the script. It's massaged by the actors, lightly changed, or a little idea will occur which will change it, or a few lines will be added.*

[Andrew Sachs] *We were a real team, as I remember it. We were able to voice whatever we felt, and all suggestions were considered, some accepted and some rejected. That's what I like about my profession, you work with others and put something together like a recipe, and everyone makes their own contribution. You may be playing the scene with another actor which then helps your own performance. It's a union…a little family.*

The term 'support' does not just relate to the actors, however. A key ingredient in the success of Laurel and Hardy films was the support provided by the team of people behind the camera. Mention has already been made of the faculties of writing, editing, and shooting but one role that hasn't been discussed is that of director. In cinema today – albeit not as much in television – the director is the main creative engine in any project but on the Laurel and Hardy set, things were very different.

Stan Laurel didn't officially direct any of the Laurel and Hardy films but, in truth, he pulled more creative strings than anybody else. In their time at Roach, Laurel and Hardy were directed by over 20 different people and yet the films show no real stylistic difference. The adjective that probably best characterises the directors chosen by Hal Roach to work with Laurel and Hardy is malleable.

Stan Laurel was never bossy or supercilious, but he had a way of making suggestions to directors without offending them or causing them to lose face. And these directors had the sense to take his suggestions in good faith for the betterment of the picture. And, in all this time, Stan never sought to be credited as a director. He had no ego in this regard; he simply wanted to make sure that the films were as good as they could be. Director of *Trailer Park Boys*, Mike Clattenburg, was similar.

[John Dunsworth] *Most directors that I've worked with are phonies. They get to where they get to for a lot of other reasons aside from talent or vision. And they copy. Phoney is maybe not the right word; I think 'poseur' is better. They play director and make sure they act like a director on the set instead of getting the goods. Mike is not playing at all; he just is. And he will stay with it until he gets it.*

Everyone in the Laurel and Hardy crew adhered to the same exacting standards and, as John Dunsworth puts it, stayed at it until it was right. This attention to detail is yet another necessary mark of great comedy.

[Tony Robinson] *There was an enormous sense of attention to detail when we were working on* Blackadder. *I've never met such a bunch of anally retentive people. Every single line, every single prop, every single writing change, every single piece of characterisation was constantly put under scrutiny in order to try and make it better. I wouldn't have wanted it any other way. Was it enjoyable? Yes it was, but it was enjoyable in a very serious way. It was work that we enjoyed and inspired us. We enjoyed the other people's work more than our own; we were all hypercritical.*

Hal Roach deserves huge credit in the Laurel and Hardy story for both demanding and facilitating excellence in the team around him. Like all great businessmen, he had the vision to employ people to do the things that he couldn't do himself and then let them get on with it.

[Graham Linehan] *On* Father Ted, *we were able to do exactly what was in our minds. People trusted us because we were Irish and it was Irish subject matter, so English producers would generally leave us to it. And the writing of it was a joy. It was such great fun coming up with the ideas because we would just sit together and make each other laugh all day.*

This joy also seems to have been experienced by the team of people working on the Laurel and Hardy films. Reports from that time talk of hard work, mutual respect, and lots of laughter. When you see the results, it's impossible to think that it could have been any other way.

8. Rise & Fall

The demise of Laurel and Hardy – for it was a demise, not a gracious retirement – is often recounted, but usually too simply. It's true that they ended their careers in abject frustration with the big studios, at the mercy of people who had no understanding of their craft, but this masks another demise, one that all comedies undergo.

The sequence of events began with the rift that started to grow between Stan Laurel and Hal Roach in the latter half of the 1930s. Now making only feature films, Roach was gambling larger sums of money on fewer pictures and so became more concerned with how these films turned out. Coupled with this, making longer films was much more difficult and these two things together prompted greater interference from the studio head.

Stan's creative control diminished. He yearned to be able to write and produce his own films, as Chaplin had done, and he began to think beyond the perimeter of Hal Roach's small Culver City studio. He knew, now, that he could work only with Oliver Hardy but the two men were employed by Roach on separate, non-concurrent contracts, so they were never free at the same time to negotiate terms as a team. However, after multiple disputes in 1938, one of which resulted in Stan Laurel being sacked by the studio – an action that was later revoked – the two comedians set themselves up as a production company and negotiated a new one-year deal with Roach.

Interestingly, the plan was to make a quartet of four-reel pictures over the coming year which Roach labeled 'streamliners.' These would be around 40 minutes long and would strip away all the plot-padding that so encumbered films like *The Bohemian Girl* (1935) and *Swiss Miss* (1938). There was something of a rebound from the trend towards double-feature programmes because of their occasional excessive length, and many exhibitors were now seeking shorter feature films.

Two pictures were made under this agreement in 1939, *A Chump at Oxford* and *Saps at Sea*, but in the end, both were stretched well beyond the four-reel plan. The other two pictures were never started and early the following year, Laurel and Hardy opted to terminate their 14-year collaboration with Hal Roach.

It is hard to believe, now, that the big studios weren't falling over themselves to sign Laurel and Hardy but at the time there was a movement towards a more quick-fire verbal style of humour, as exemplified by Bob Hope, Abbott and Costello, Red Skelton, and Danny Kaye. The studio executives at 20th Century Fox did at least realise that there was still a market for what was beginning to be seen as passé, slapstick humour, but what they failed to appreciate was that Laurel and Hardy's comedy had a subtlety and delicacy that distinguished it. And although the big studios had money to spend, they hadn't the least idea how to spend it. And worse, they had a production-line way of doing things which quashed creativity and relegated Stan Laurel from a role of all-around creator to that of jobbing actor.

Between 1941 and 1945, Laurel and Hardy made six films for 20th Century-Fox and two for MGM, and faced the same frustrations in all of them. Writers were assigned who had little comedy-writing experience and a poor knowledge of Laurel and Hardy. Equally inappropriate choices were made for the director's chair and these men, unlike those at Roach, weren't in the habit of seeking advice from the cast. Tellingly, the initial scripts and the final films were almost identical; there appears to have been no scope for ad-libbing or the redevelopment of scenes on-set that had characterised their greatest work at Roach. And, crucially, there was a briskness in how the films were made and a lack of attention to detail. Hal Roach always had to distribute his movies through a larger player – usually

MGM – so he developed a habit of striving for quality, but Fox had their own distribution network of over 500 cinemas, meaning that whatever they made got shown, no matter how poor it was.

You could talk with righteous incredulity about the stupidity and insensitivity of the big studio treatment of the greatest comedy double act of all time. You could lambaste the young writer at MGM who never bothered to watch any of Laurel and Hardy's films, stating glibly, 'They were a comedy team and I was an established comedy writer; that was all there was to it. There was no such thing as research back then.' And you could isolate lines of dialogue, like this one from Oliver Hardy: 'It's better to spend one night with a corpse than 60 days with the cops!' and ask: who the hell is this supposed to be? But it is a waste of time and energy to do so. The simplest and most pertinent thing you can say about the six films Laurel and Hardy made for 20th Century Fox and the two they made for MGM is that they were awful.

Stan Laurel was not a bitter person, but he was extremely bitter about this.

[Stan Laurel] *We had some very bad experiences after leaving Roach. With Roach, we had more freedom; we could make it how we wanted. With the other places, like Metro and 20th Century Fox, the story was written, cut and dried, and it had to be shot per script. And the routines and gags were all what we had previously done and the story behind them didn't permit us to get the best out of them. It was a disgusting affair to us all the way through, so we were happy when the contract was called off.*

This story – the move from short films to features; the ensuing rift with Hal Roach; the falling from favour of visual comedy; the relegation of the Stan and Ollie characters to that of stooges in poorly made, big-studio B-movies – has a clean arc to it, but these events hide something else. With comedy, there is an indefinable blend of conditions that coalesce and allow something to bloom, but as mysteriously and as quickly as a great comedy comes to thrive, it also comes to wither and die. And although it's true that everything runs out of steam eventually, comedy seems particularly fragile in this regard. So it may be reasonable to ask, notwithstanding their mauling by the big studios, whether Laurel and Hardy had not already passed their best.

There is a strange process whereby, over time, comedies grow self-conscious and less assured. It is as if they become caricatures of their former selves and the humour becomes forced.

[Ardal O'Hanlon] *They lose that adrenaline, I think, and people become complacent. It's inevitable. Or they simply run out of ideas and inspiration.*

It seems that comedy is not so amenable to coercion and the writers of many of the greatest sitcoms have solved this problem by simply avoiding it.

[Graham Linehan] *The worst thing is the series too far. It happens in America all the time. They just can't help it because their seasons are so long and eventually they have no choice but to jump the shark. For example,* Seinfeld *was glorious for about five or six seasons, maybe seven at a stretch, but eventually it became the silliest, most embarrassing collection of dreadfully self-aware moments.* Fawlty Towers *had absolutely the right idea: get in, make your comedy quick and then get out before anybody grows bored of you. Don't do one series too many, do one series too few, and people will always love you.*

There are many examples of great sitcoms that ceased trading long before the viewing public got tired of them. There were only two series of *Fawlty Towers*, three of *Father Ted*, three of *Blackadder* (following the alterations made after series one), two of *The Office*, and two of *The Young Ones*.

Before leaving Roach, Laurel and Hardy had made 71 short films, and 14 feature films, which, by comedy standards, is a pretty good innings. And it is remarkable just how many of these films – the shorts in particular – stand up today. However, it could be argued that the five films they made after *Way Out West* in 1937 – before going to 20th Century Fox – display a greater sense of silliness and a more laboured attempt to play the characters directly for laughs.

An interesting indication of this is the way that Stan's character becomes more voluble in later films. If you look at the early talking shorts – for example *Night Owls* (1929) or *Hog Wild* (1930) – and do a simple word count for Stan over the film's 20-minute duration, the totals are remarkably low: 38 and 35 words respectively. To put this into context, there are 142 words in this paragraph alone. Indeed, if you take all Stan's lines in *Night Owls* – if you could call them lines – and compile them into a single sound recording, he speaks all his dialogue in just 12 seconds. However, if you do a similar word count for the first 20 minutes of *The Flying Deuces* (1939), Stan's total is a garrulous 730 words. By the end of the decade, it seems, he has become 20-times more talkative.

Obviously, characters undergo subtle changes with time and in the early days of sound, Laurel and Hardy were probably under-utilising dialogue, but there is still a beautiful simplicity to these early films that gets swamped somewhat by verbal gags in the latter days at Roach. And even their visual humour had changed over the years, becoming slightly more pronounced and deliberate: in the way they walked, in the way they swung their arms, in the way they banged their heads, in the general pacing of the action. Coupled with this, in 1940, Stan Laurel was 50 years of age and Oliver Hardy was 48, and slapstick is obviously a young man's game. Even with a more sympathetic employer than Fox or MGM, it is hard to see how much further they could have gone at the standards they had set for themselves.

There was never really any question of them changing their on-screen personas or taking things in a new direction.

Characters as well known as Laurel and Hardy would probably never have been allowed to be anybody else; comedy tends to brand people in this regard more possessively than anything else. Once you have made people laugh, you will be asked to do so again and again, as Harry H. Corbett found out, despite the huge promise he showed as a straight actor in his brief career before *Steptoe & Son*.

[Galton & Simpson] *Later on, Harry tried to do a bit of straight acting, but I think the only one that really worked was called* Rattle of the Simple Man, *where he was basically playing* Steptoe *but in the North of England. Harry had this vocal thing where everything he did sounded like Harry H. Corbett. And I think one of the reasons he was hailed as such a wonderful actor was because of his unusual delivery; he gave unusual twists to things. It seemed to me that everything he did after* Steptoe, *sounded like* Steptoe. *He never did anything straight successfully afterwards.*

Corbett created such a unique character that he couldn't escape him. The same was true of Stan Laurel, although he didn't feel encumbered by this in the same way. It had taken him a long time to find this special chemistry with Hardy and he never seemed to tire of the situation. In fact, even after the Hardy's death in 1957, Stan Laurel often imagined new ideas for Laurel and Hardy films. It is amazing that they developed such strong archetypes given the backdrop of fast-paced slapstick from which they hailed.

[Stephen Merchant] *One of the things that I admire about them so hugely is the fact that they ever managed to create such a sophisticated pair of characters. It's all the more admirable, in a way, because when we came to write the character of David Brent, he came pretty much out of the box. There was a long tradition of comedy that pre-existed* The Office *that you can look to as a guide. We were always able to look back and see how the mechanics worked. But what's so extraordinary about Laurel and Hardy is that there isn't anyone prior to them as a precedent.*

Laurel and Hardy finished with the big studios in 1945, and it's probably not unreasonable to ask why they did not do so sooner. It is suggested that Stan thought if he could stick things out, he might start to gain more control. In this kind of limbo, and with both men under considerable alimony pressures, four years could probably pass quite quickly. We can all doubtless look at chunks of our own lives and ask the question: what was I doing all that time?

They embarked on the first of three very successful stage tours of Britain in 1947, but they did have one more outing on film in 1950. Recognising their huge popularity in Europe, an American financier, George Bookbinder, pulled together a British, Italian, French and American consortium to make a Laurel and Hardy film in France, which would become known as *Atoll K*. It was one of the sorriest of sorry last outings that any former great in any field has had to endure. If the films at Fox and MGM suffered from an excess of control, *Atoll K* suffered from its complete absence.

There were multiple writers, multiple directors, multiple languages and multiple visions on how the project should progress. And, largely because Stan Laurel fell seriously ill at this time, the project hardly progressed at all. Twelve weeks of shooting extended to 12 months and the final product was feeble. Even with huge personal interest in all things Laurel and Hardy, I could only watch 15 minutes of *Atoll K*, and not because I found it demeaning or sad, but simply because it was so poor.

[Stan Laurel] *We had three nationalities and of course their sense of humour was entirely different. Then we came to shoot and no one knew what anyone was talking about and we were hoping we were answering the right questions* [laughs]. *And on top of that, I got very ill and ended up weighing 114 lbs having been 160, so I could hardly stand up to finish the picture. It was a mess all the way around, just unfortunate. We were a bit embarrassed over it.*

Oliver Hardy lived until 1957; Stan Laurel until 1965. At the end of his days, Stan spent his time replying to fan mail, watching television, and entertaining the frequent visitors to his Santa Monica apartment. Interestingly, one such pilgrim bridges the gap between the era of silent comedy and that of modern sitcom.

[Galton & Simpson] *Hancock met Stan Laurel. We didn't inquire too deeply about it because I don't think we were speaking to Tony at the time, but he did say he went to visit him and he was charming and lived very modestly. I always remember him saying that the thing that galled Stan Laurel most was that all the films had been edited for children's television in America and all the good bits, to his mind, had been cut out. All the slapstick and the custard pies had been kept in and all the little nuances had been removed, and of course he could do nothing about it.*

It must have been hard for Stan Laurel to see his life's work treated with such a lack of respect and understanding.

[Stan Laurel] *I'm so disappointed with the way they're edited, and the commercials are stuck in here and there in the middle of a gag…the questions are cut out and the answers are just given and you don't know what it's all about. So I lost interest in looking at them.*

Stan Laurel might have felt, from what he was seeing on television, that comedy tastes were moving on. But as the contributors to this book attest, it is the early days of American television that have dated and not the films that Stan Laurel helped to make with such care and affection. He may have been aware of, and overwhelmed by, their popularity up to that time, but he could surely have little guessed that their comedy would have endured so strongly into the next century.

9. Endurance

Despite the best sitcoms attracting huge television audiences, and taking up such a significant place in the public's imagination, comedy is never taken as seriously as other genres.

[Graham Linehan] *We're sitting at the children's table, really, with sitcom. People don't take us as seriously as they would take playwrights, for example. You have to learn to live with that and not moan about it too much, or you'd go crazy. In the end, I suppose you've got to have some perspective because you're writing a little half-hour thing that comes on before* Wife Swap.

The truth is, sitcoms are incredibly difficult to do, as evidenced by the dearth of good sitcoms today. Over the last five decades, the flow of good television comedies has been little more than a trickle. And this has always been the case, as Oliver Hardy recognised in 1950.

[Oliver Hardy] *I think there is more interest in the old slapstick material, but there is so little of it done. I think people want to laugh, now, but they don't have the things to laugh at. People nowadays want to be connected with the higher type of drama and they don't want to be associated with comedy. That's because comedy is difficult to make, you see.*

Many great writers have followed roaring hit with inexplicable flop, a hazard not nearly so common among novelists and playwrights. And when comedies do work, there seems to be an element of accident, an inexplicable ingredient that differentiates the funny from the forgettable. The idea for *Steptoe & Son* came on a whim in a near desperate brainstorming session for Galton and Simpson's new series, *Comedy Playhouse*. This featured a different situation each week, and the writers had run aground on episode four. The suggestion of two rag-and-bone men was made, rejected, and then revisited several unproductive hours after. And even when the episode had been written, shot, and very well received by the public, there were no plans to take it any further.

[Galton & Simpson] *We weren't interested, and we found every excuse in the book not to write a series because we thought, after ten years of Hancock, that's enough. Now we'd got our own show, we became the stars and we could write what we liked. And although that was hard because we had nothing to fall back on each week, it allowed us to work with actors, not comedians. So we made all the excuses in the world not to do a series and our last excuse was: if Harry [H. Corbett] and Willy [Brambell] want to do it, we'll do it…thinking they won't. And they jumped at it.*

As we saw, it was similar forces of chance that brought Laurel and Hardy together. Several people can duly be credited with spotting the on-screen rapport when it appeared, and then doing what was necessary to nurture it, but even Stan was mystified by just how popular the team's films would become in the end.

[Stan Laurel] *It's remarkable, the love that they have for us. It's amazing. Still today* [1957] *they take about three of our two-reelers and put them together, and those pictures run for five or six months in one house. I have recently received letters to this effect from Germany and different places. And it's the only picture showing and they stand in line.*

One incident that illustrates not just their popularity, but also the love the public felt for Laurel and Hardy, is the famous Cobh story from 1953. On the way to the UK for their third stage tour, they were moored off Cobh on the south coast of Ireland and word had reached the town that Laurel and Hardy were on board. People swarmed along the quayside.

[Stan Laurel] *It's a strange, strange thing. Our last good pictures were made in the thirties, and you'd think people would forget, but they don't. The love and affection we found that day at Cobh was simply unbelievable. There were hundreds of boats blowing whistles and mobs and mobs of people screaming on the docks. We just couldn't understand what it was all about. And then something* *happened that I can never forget. All the church bells in Cobh started to ring out our theme song and Babe looked at me and we cried. Maybe people loved us and our pictures because we put so much love in them. I don't know. I'll never forget that day, never.*

One of the great things about the Laurel and Hardy legacy is the fact that they appealed to an audience that ranged in age from three to 93. Indeed, most people who have come to love their films started to develop a relationship with them at a very early age.

[Ardal O'Hanlon] *They used to show them on Saturday mornings and we used to watch them religiously and absolutely love them.*

[Stephen Merchant] *It's slightly difficult for me to remove them from the nostalgia I have for when my father and I used to watch them when I was younger. It might be harder to discover them later in life. That's not to say that the comedy is immature, but there's something about them that probably got under my skin when I was young. In a way, I've appreciated them differently at different stages in my life.*

This might lead you to wonder if they would be as funny to somebody who came upon them later in their life, but Andrew Sachs provides an interesting and untypical counter-example.

[Andrew Sachs] *When I watched them on Saturday mornings as a boy, I was never that keen. I thought they were slow and I didn't take to them particularly. But I grew to admire and respect them, funnily enough, after I got married. My wife has always been a great fan and I couldn't quite see it, but then she made me watch them and I have to agree with her [laughing], they are rather brilliant.*

Whatever the age that people first happen on Laurel and Hardy, it is certainly true that people do not tire of them when they grow up. If anything, the opposite happens.

[Ardal O'Hanlon] *About two years ago I bought the box set and introduced them to my children, who were about seven or eight at the time. They really got into it, which is very gratifying because you're* *always wary about revisiting your comic heroes; you're afraid that it won't stand up and it definitely did. I was amazed, even the black and white, which kids are so resistant to nowadays, never bothered them. Laurel and Hardy are such strong archetypal characters. And even one night, recently, an hour before they went to bed, I asked them what they wanted to watch, and they said Laurel and Hardy. Which is great. I'm delighted; it gives me an excuse to look at them as well.*

[Nigel Planer] *I watched them as a kid. Although I can now appreciate Chaplin and the others, at the time, the only ones that I could get into were Laurel and Hardy. And when I had kids of my own, they hooked up with them as well.*

It seems any generation that has been given the chance to enjoy Laurel and Hardy has done so.

[Bruce Forsyth] *I was in the Imperial Hotel in Blackpool, in the days when they didn't have a television in each room, which just shows you how far back it was, and I saw in the paper that Laurel and Hardy were on TV. It was one of their short films, so I came down to the lounge and there were about 12 kids running around and playing. They weren't really watching the television and I said to one of them, 'Oh, do you mind if I switch this over?' and he said, 'Well we're watching such-and-such,' and I said, 'No you're not, you're all playing.' Well, this went on until finally I said, 'Well, it will only be on for about 20 minutes, and I'm going to watch it.' And I switched it over and after about five minutes, all these kids who had been running around, were all sitting down watching Laurel and Hardy. And I thought to myself, they will always have an audience.*

Today, however, timeless audience or not, television stations are showing Laurel and Hardy less and less often. There can be little doubt that they still have unprecedented appeal, but in order to sell this to the next generation, a certain bravery and open-mindedness is required on the part of the broadcasters.

[Stephen Merchant] *I think, to get kids watching them, you need to show, maybe, two at once…a double-bill of short films, because, as with a lot of good comedy, you need to get used to it, you* *need to understand the dynamic. Once that affection has grown, then it becomes funnier.*

It may be that their recent absence from our screens is just one of the pendulum swings of fashion. Certainly, many comedians who were considered stale and old-fashioned 20 years ago have since been heralded as legends. However, even if it is just fashion, it is impossible to predict if, or when, broadcasters will deem Laurel and Hardy to be 'in' once more.

[Ardal O'Hanlon] *When* The Office *came out, everyone probably thought, 'Oh my god, we've got to do the more naturalistic style…without an audience…single camera…edgy,' and that was a trend for a while. But now television companies are actually looking for prime-time sitcoms. It seems that they do want the old conventional type again.*

It would be wrong, given the interest shown in this book, to say that Laurel and Hardy are sliding from public consciousness. As far back as 1940, this seemed to be a concern and yet I managed to grow up with Laurel and Hardy nearly four decades later. There is, after all, a timeless realism to them and something pure and universal about their humour. Maybe comedy of the very silliest kind, on the rare occasions when it is done well, taps into something universal.

[Graham Linehan] *With* Father Ted, *we would always take it as a compliment when somebody said, 'Oh, that's completely stupid.' It was partly because, in the early nineties, we were such big fans of Vic Reeves and Bob Mortimer, and we were aiming for something completely idiotic, for jokes that weren't satire or parody, but jokes that were just…funny. There's an argument that this is the purest form of comedy. I would put something like Steve Martin's early stand-up in that category. He is a very intelligent man but his funniest comedy is incredibly stupid.*

There is nothing analytical, satirical, or political about the Laurel and Hardy films; they are simply about very ordinary people going about their very ordinary business, and coming unstuck. Maybe this is one of the reasons why even if the crackly film has dated a little, the comedy has not.

[Barry Cryer] *The comedy performers that last were never topical. There are brilliant, satirical comedians who have their time and then they're out of fashion, but the likes of Morecambe and Wise and Tommy Cooper are completely timeless. Like Laurel and Hardy. They just do the eternals; they make it look so easy; it's boiling comedy down to absolute basics.*

Thankfully we can enjoy the 'eternals' of Laurel and Hardy as nearly all of their films are available in good condition which, ironically, cannot be said of many classic sitcoms made several decades later. This was the case with the so-called 'Lost Steptoes'.

[Galton & Simpson] *The sad thing is that both series [series five and six] were in colour and the BBC usually only repeat colour, they don't repeat black and white if they can help it. We had them all recorded privately but only in black and white. We arranged for one of the societies to transfer them back onto film.*

In those days, they didn't save things like they do now. They didn't know that there was going to be a great future for recorded programmes. Jim Perry [who wrote Dad's Army*] was saying recently that they didn't save things because they were all recorded on a system called Ampex, and each tape cost £600 which back then was a great deal of money. So they would re-use the tapes. When we started with* Hancock, *they didn't even record the programmes. They had a system of retaining selected episodes. If you had a series of 20, they might save four for the archives. But they didn't have a policy of saving everything like they do now.*

One obstacle that may obstruct future generations from growing up with Laurel and Hardy is the length of their films. Black and white pictures are frequently shown on television and are an accepted part of the schedule, but these are always feature films; short films are harder to place. And it is the short films that represent the best of

Laurel and Hardy, a point on which Stan Laurel was emphatic.

[Stan Laurel] *We should have stayed in the short film category. There is just so much comedy we can do along a certain line and then it gets to be unfunny. You can't take a whole series of things we do, stick them all together in eight reels and expect to get a well-balanced picture out of it. We didn't want to go into feature films in the first place and even though I've got some favourites among them, I'm sorry we ever did go beyond the two- and three-reelers.*

Unusually, though, Stan seems to contradict this statement in a later taped interview. Here, when asked which films he considered to be the team's best, he gave this answer:

[Stan Laurel] *Well, I think one of our best was* Fra Diavolo, *another cute picture was* Bonnie Scotland…Babes in Toyland…*and I liked* The Bohemian Girl.

These are all feature films and, aside from the fact that he didn't mention most people's favourite, *Sons of the Desert*, it is strange that he didn't cite any shorts. Maybe he felt that the question inherently implied feature films as these titles might be more memorable in the public consciousness. But this just reinforces the idea that the short films seem to be considered somehow less important and therefore less repeat-worthy.

I have seen all the short films on television, most of them many times. I have also managed to record all these films on VHS from television, at one time or another, so easy were they to net. However, in the last ten years, TV screenings of Laurel and Hardy have all but ceased.

Television can be quite conservative in this regard. Like nightclubs that won't play music without a beat, even the dedicated comedy channels tend to broadcast only modern shows, many of which don't seem terribly funny to me. It is interesting to reflect that so many of the top names in comedy today, whose own work does get aired frequently, would themselves far rather be watching Laurel and Hardy than most of what is shown.

[Richard Wilson] *For me, no one can beat them. It was this extraordinary mixture they had of pathos, cruelty and blind timing. I don't often sit down to watch them but if I come across them and dip in, I still laugh, even though I know the films. The times you do catch a snatch on the telly, you just start laughing immediately. I can't think of any performers who have lasted so long and still work.*

You could call this the stop-and-smile phenomenon and it infects most people who have even a passing regard for Laurel and Hardy. Of which there are many.

[Bruce Forsyth] *They were my favourite. I absolutely adored them, from a child right through. If there was a Laurel and Hardy film on at the moment, I'd have to tell you to call back later. No matter where I am, if Laurel and Hardy are on, I have to stop and watch because I just adore them.*

We can only hope that Laurel and Hardy appear more on television in the future because the anecdotal evidence is overwhelming: if the viewers are introduced to them at an early age, they will come to love them. It is a promise often made and more frequently true of Laurel and Hardy than most: 'I want you to meet a couple of friends of mine, I'm sure you will love them.'

10. Last Laugh

[Stephen Merchant] Favourite Film: *Chickens Come Home*. (A former girlfriend of Ollie's comes back to blackmail him, after he has – rather implausibly – become rich and successful. Stan is given the job of keeping her at bay while Ollie entertains guests.)

Favourite Set-up: *I love ones where they are in an infrastructure that is then upset. What I love about* Chickens Come Home, *as well as many others, is that prior to the film, life is going along fine. Ollie is the owner of a company, he has a big house and a wife, and Stan is one of the employees. And yet, strangely, when the camera is turned on, the tragedy begins. There's something at stake, a marriage, a job, and then they've got to do something simple and they just can't manage it. I also love the fact that they're sexualised as humans; they're men, even though they're men acting like children. Something about that makes them more real.*

[Tony Robinson] Favourite Film: *I couldn't say.*

Favourite Set-up: *I prefer it when it's just them in their ordinary lives solving a very simple problem. Strip everything else away except the two guys in their little hats solving a problem.*

Why were they so well loved: *There's only one word that comes to mind and that's tenderness.*

[Nigel Planer] Favourite Film: *The one where they have to deliver a piano* [The Music Box]. *And the one where they slowly dismantle a house and the man whose house it is slowly dismantles their car* [Big Business]…*I find that one very funny indeed.*

Favourite Set-up: *I do like it when they have wives but if you were going for the pure essence of it, it's better when they are stuck on one little thing like trying to deliver a piano…just one event that is completely impossible for them. It's also quite nice, I suppose, when* *the wives are there at the beginning and say something like, 'I'm going out now, you better not mess up the kitchen,' and then they mess up the kitchen. Put them in any single situation and watch it develop.*

[Richard Wilson] Favourite Film: *That's a tough one. I think* Blockheads *stands out a bit, but I've never thought of having a favourite, it's just anything they do. In fact, now that I've talked to you, I must go out and buy some of the DVDs.*

Favourite Set-up: *I think it would be just them going for a trip to the seaside, something as simple as possible. They'd do a brilliant job of making it real.*

[Ardal O'Hanlon] Favourite Film: *I do like* Way Out West, *although I've seen it far too many times. It's one of the kids' favourites. But I think I'd have to plump for* Blockheads. *There's just that amazing scene where Ollie goes to collect Stan from the hospital and he thinks he's lost a leg and is carrying him everywhere. It's brilliant and there are so many moments like that throughout their careers, just brilliant, brilliant moments.*

Favourite Set-up: *The two of them in an Antarctic research station; I think that would be quite interesting. Or a parochial house on a remote island off the coast of Ireland. There was one short where they were playing bell-hops in a hotel; I'd like to see that developed a bit more.*

[Bruce Forsyth] Favourite Film: *I like so many of them. And even now, if one comes on, it might be one I haven't seen because they made so many. I think my favourite feature film was* A Chump at Oxford. *That was brilliant and very clever…the way Stan kept going back to being the idiot. I laugh when I think of it now.* (Stan and Ollie accidentally foil a bank raid and are rewarded with scholarships to Oxford. Stan bangs his head and regains his former identity as the surprisingly intelligent, Hardy-baiting Lord Paddington.)

Favourite Set-up: *I love it when they are married and if they're going to do something they know is a bit naughty, Ollie says, 'And we don't have to tell our wives.' I'm laughing just thinking about it.*

[Barry Cryer] *Favourite Film:* *I don't have a favourite one – I'm quite indiscriminate with them, particularly the shorter ones. Of course, I have favourite moments:* Blue Ridge Mountains of Virginia *and some of their dancing routines. I know that's a very obvious choice but the way the film stops while they do that decorous dance is just sheer joy. I haven't got a favourite film because there are favourite scenes that they do in all of their films, so I could watch any of them.*

Favourite Set-up: *I would like the wives there because it's so funny with Ollie posing in front of the women and Stan running scared...oh yes, I'd definitely have the wives there.*

[Andrew Sachs] *Favourite Film:* *Of course there is the famous one with the piano. But I remember bits more than I remember films. The way Oliver Hardy uses the camera to bring the audience into the situation is lovely and he doesn't overdo it. And the thinking time that goes on between the two of them. Those are the elements of their humour that I particularly appreciate.*

[Galton & Simpson] *Favourite Film*: *The one that used to make us laugh like mad was the one with Jimmy Finlayson where they're selling Christmas trees in California* [Big Business]. *They destroy his house and he destroys their car. He finishes with the car but they have quite a bit to go on his house and he doesn't know what to do next, so he has a go at their Christmas trees and the trees just bend and there's this wonderful frustration. Also,* County Hospital. *There was the line, 'Hard-Boiled Eggs and Nuts' which we used as an homage in two of our own shows. Also* A Chump at Oxford *and* Way Out West.

Favourite Set-up: *Ray Galton: I did always like it when they were trying to get away from their terrible wives. Alan Simpson: I think I prefer the ones where they were on their own. I don't* *particularly like to think of them being married, I think of them as being married to each other.*

[Graham Linehan] Favourite Film: *I don't know why but the one where they're on a boat and Laurel gets his head stuck behind the mast* [Towed in a Hole]; *that's a big one for me. And of course the one where they're moving the piano* [The Music Box].

Favourite Set-up: *I like anything where they are near dangerous machinery, woodcutters or working on a chimney…anything where there's real physical danger, and the worse the danger, the funnier it will be. I think the best thing would be a factory from the thirties or forties, where things are beginning to get mechanised but the safety laws aren't really in place. That would be good.*

Filmography

(Length of feature films given in minutes. For short films, two reels is just under 20 minutes. The year cited is the one in which the film was shot. All films made at the Hal Roach Studios, except where noted.)

Silent Films

1919

Lucky Dog – two reels, Bronco Billy Anderson

1926

Duck Soup – two reels
Slipping Wives – two reels

1927

Love 'Em & Weep – two reels
Why Girls Love Sailors – two reels
With Love & Hisses – two reels
Sailors Beware – two reels
Do Detectives Think? – two reels
Flying Elephants – two reels
Sugar Daddies – two reels
The Second Hundred Years – two reels
Hats Off – two reels
Putting Pants on Philip – two reels
The Battle of the Century – two reels
Leave 'Em Laughing – two reels
The Finishing Touch – two reels
From Soup to Nuts – two reels

1928

You're Darn Tootin' – two reels
Their Purple Moment – two reels
Should Married Men Go Home? – two reels
Early to Bed – two reels
Two Tars – two reels
Habeas Corpus – two reels
We Faw Down – two reels
Liberty – two reels
Wrong Again – two reels
That's My Wife – two reels
Big Business – two reels

1929

Double Whoopee – two reels
Bacon Grabbers – two reels
Angora Love – two reels

Sound Films

1929

Unaccustomed As We Are – two reels
Berth Marks – two reels
Men O' War – two reels
Perfect Day – two reels
They Go Boom – two reels
The Hoose-Gow – two reels
Night Owls – two reels

Blotto – two reels

1930

Brats – two reels
Below Zero – two reels
Hog Wild – two reels
The Laurel and Hardy Murder Case – two reels
Pardon Us – 56 minutes
Another Fine Mess – two reels
Be Big – two reels

1931

Chickens Come Home – two reels
Laughing Gravy – two reels
Our Wife – two reels
Come Clean – two reels
One Good Turn – two reels
Beau Hunks – four reels
Helpmates – two reels
Any Old Port – two reels
The Music Box – three reels

1932

The Chimp – three reels
County Hospital – two reels
Pack Up Your Troubles – 68 minutes
Scram – two reels
Their First Mistake – two reels

Towed in a Hole – two reels
Twice Two – two reels

1933

Fra Diavalo – 90 minutes
Me & My Pal – two reels
The Midnight Patrol – two reels
Busy Bodies – two reels
Dirty Work – two reels
Sons of the Desert – 68 minutes

1934

Oliver the Eighth – three reels
Going Bye Bye – two reels
Them Thar Hills – two reels
Babes in Toyland – 79 minutes
The Live Ghost – two reels
Tit for Tat – two reels

1935

The Fixer Uppers – two reels
Bonnie Scotland – 80 minutes
Thicker Than Water – two reels
The Bohemian Girl – 70 minutes

1936

Our Relations – 74 minutes
Way Out West – 65 minutes

1938

Swiss Miss – 72 minutes

Block-Heads – 58 minutes

1939

A Chump at Oxford – 63 minutes (Europe), 42 minutes (USA)

The Flying Deuces – 69 minutes, Morros/RKO

Saps at Sea – 57 minutes

1941

Great Guns – 74 minutes, 20th Century-Fox

1942

A-Haunting We Will Go – 67 minutes, 20th Century-Fox

Air Raid Wardens – 67 minutes, MGM

1943

Jitterbugs – 74 minutes, 20th Century-Fox

The Dancing Masters – 63 minutes, 20th Century-Fox

1944

The Big Noise – 74 minutes, 20th Century-Fox

Nothing But Trouble – 70 minutes, MGM

The Bullfighters – 69 minutes, 20th Century-Fox

1951

Atoll K – 82 minutes, Sirius/Fortezza

Bibliography

Laurel and Hardy – The Magic Behind the Movies, Randy Skredvedt, Moonstone Press, USA, 1987

Mr Laurel and Mr Hardy, John McCabe, Robson Books, London 1976

Stan, Fred Lawrence Guiles, Michael Joseph, London, 1980

The World of Laurel and Hardy, Thomas Leeflang, Windward, Leicester, 1988

The Laurel and Hardy Digest, Willie McIntyre, Willie McIntyre, Scotland, 1998

The Life and Times of Laurel and Hardy, Ronald Bergin, Green Wood, London, 1992

Stan and Ollie – The Roots of Comedy, Simon Louvish, Faber and Faber, London, 2001

Epilogue

Stephen Merchant, at six foot seven, is hard to miss. I spotted him at chucking out time in a pub in Hampstead on a weekend trip from Dublin to visit my brother who was living in London at the time. I had the idea for a book based on a set of interviews with famous Laurel and Hardy fans but, having done plenty of research and compiled a long wish-list of comedy actors and writers I wanted to talk to, I had no idea how to make a start. So seeing Stephen Merchant was a twist of fate that left me with no reasonable choice but to do something I would normally never do: doorstep him.

He was very courteous and seemed to take on board the one-minute spiel I ran past him which I'd concocted just one minute before. He suggested I contact his agent – I knew nothing of 'talent agents' or 'representation' then – so I had my first tangible target although, to be honest, I didn't expect him to say yes.

A few days later I got an email from a 'Katie':

> **Hi Barry, Steve can do this on the phone. When is your deadline?**

My deadline, as things turned out, would end up being some years in the future, but this was the start that made everything else possible. Stephen Merchant was on *The Graham Norton Show* later that week promoting the *Extras* Christmas special, so he didn't need to be talking to me. But he did. And this was the case with nearly all of the contributors; there was a real love for Laurel and Hardy, more than I could have imagined.

Stephen Merchant is self-effacing, interesting, and interested. Philosophical, in ways, but also funny, articulate, and sharp. In other words, my first interview was extremely easy and enjoyable. When I listen back on it,

I'm surprised by how stupidly unhurried I was but, in fairness, Stephen was in no way impatient or irked.

*

Someone asked me, after I'd interviewed him, what **Bruce Forsyth** was like. 'He's just the way you'd think him to be,' I said. Then I thought about this and corrected myself. 'He's just the way you'd *like* to think he *would* be.' In other words, his warmth, sincerity, and humour are not an act.

I didn't think I'd get to speak with him, partly because he is such an A-lister but also because the timing was so bad. He was presenting *Strictly Come Dancing* and he had just turned 80, so there was a television special and you can only imagine how many private functions and get-togethers. But Ian, his agent, although as tough as you'd guess a top star's agent should be, kept saying little things which led me to believe Bruce actually wanted to do the interview but just couldn't. Yet.

By small degrees, it started to look more and more likely before, some months and many phone calls and emails from my first enquiry, I finally got to talk to him. And despite all this build-up and having seen Bruce Forsyth on television pretty much non-stop for as long as I could remember, it was as easy as having coffee with a friend.

When he said, 'If there was a Laurel and Hardy film on at the moment, I'd have to tell you to call back later,' he laughed but I knew he probably meant it. You could tell that his love of Laurel and Hardy was absolute.

One of the most interesting things Bruce Forsyth said to me, though, only struck me a week later. It's something he has in common with Laurel and Hardy and which makes him unique among the list of contributors to this book. Nearly everything he has done professionally has been performed to a family audience. People of literally all ages, from three to 103 can engage with and enjoy his shows. And what brought this home to me was *Strictly Come Dancing* which I caught the start of the following weekend, where he introduced the show – as he always has – with the words, 'Good evening ladies, gentlemen, and children.'

*

I asked **Tony Robinson** if he saw himself as a comedian or as an actor but he didn't think it was important. Of his one-man shows, he said, 'They are probably ten percent stand-up, 40 percent observation, and 50 percent story telling. What that means I am,' he added, 'I don't know. I'm just a guy who…I'm just an entertainer.'

Which struck me as being an important point. Tony Robinson has a hugely mixed CV – actor, comedian, writer, children's entertainer, historian, presenter – and is just attracted to do what he thinks is a good thing to do, regardless of what he 'is' or has ever thought he should be. Just like Stan Laurel.

Before Stan Laurel (accidentally) teamed up with Oliver Hardy, he had moved into a director's role at Hal Roach. And even when he went on to become the actor we all came to love, he was still helping to write the films, direct them, edit them and make them as good as they could be. Tony Robinson seemed to embody the same idea, that you work towards making the whole of what you are involved in good, rather than being obsessed with your own individual part. Baldrick is a prime example. He must be one of the most understated, under-hammed, and under-forced roles in comedy. He doesn't, like many of the characters in Blackadder, make sarcastic remarks or string long pieces of elaborate language together, and yet his simple lines bring the house down. As Tony Robinson said, 'He was just there and the audience could fill in the emotions.'

*

I met **Ardal O'Hanlon** in a café in Ranelagh, Dublin, which was great because most of the other interviews were done over the phone and it's easier to converse with someone you can see. Also, you can have coffee and cake.

We talked about many things and strayed far beyond the subject of Laurel and Hardy. I asked him about his novel, *The Talk of the Town*, which I'd read and greatly enjoyed. It had surprised people with its darkness – not obvious Dougal material – and had not been a trivial undertaking for its author.

'Novel writing is such a massive commitment and it takes a toll on you, personally and psychologically and emotionally and every way. And I had a young family around the place and I couldn't keep doing that to myself in front of them, I was in too much pain trying to write.

'I did try to write a second novel, but I just couldn't get to grips with it. It was too ambitious, and a bit all over the place, and I just couldn't salvage it despite repeated attempts because I was very easily seduced by sitcoms and other work. So I said to myself, I'll leave that for another day when I don't have the options that I have now. I was still young enough to do stand up.'

I asked him about 'arse-skiing' in the novel – very funny – and Ardal told me where much of the material had come from. 'That whole book was about the craziness that I witnessed, week in, week out, when I was a 16-, 17-year-old boy going out to night clubs and stuff.

'I think there's something in the Irish psyche, and I'm sure it informs Father Ted greatly, a recklessness that I think is in me and everyone I know. I'll leave it to somebody else to go into the reasons why that is, but here there is a wildness, a wild streak, that's different to other cultures.'

There was a guy at another table shouting during this. Not in a disruptive way; he seemed to know the staff and was obviously a regular but an eccentric one. Not quite normal but harmless. Earlier he had asked me to remove the wrapper on his coffee biscuit for him and now he was departing with protracted farewells. As he passed our table he said, 'Bye, men,' to which Ardal cheerily replied, 'Bye,

bye, now.' After all the talk of 'psyches' and 'personal tolls', it was like Dougal had come back into the room.

*

I sent an interview request to **John Dunsworth**'s agent and, a few days later, received the following email from a 'Sheila'.

> **Barry Brophy,**
>
> **We have received a forwarded email from you requesting an interview with John Dunsworth. He has tried to call you at the numbers provided in the email. The numbers appear not to be working.**
>
> **Perhaps you could call him on his mobile**

God, I thought, how did I mess that up? Did I mess that up? I checked the email I'd sent and found my mobile number correctly typed but – and I don't know what made me think of this – I looked up the international dialling code from Canada to Ireland and found that it was **011** not the **00** I'd put down, which works from nearly everywhere else.

I was embarrassed about this and worried that I might have put John off, particularly as he had phoned so spontaneously. I texted an apology, an explanation of my stupidity and asked if he might still be free to talk. He told me to phone him straight back.

Of all the people I spoke to, John Dunsworth was probably least directly acquainted with Laurel and Hardy. He remembered them, certainly, but didn't have detailed knowledge of their films. So why had he been so amenable to doing the interview? Because, simply put, that's they kind of guy he is.

Unlike his *Trailer Park Boys* character, the immense Officer Jim Lahey, John Dunsworth doesn't drink. By all accounts, he rises early, retires late, and crams as much as he can into every day. His activities are varied; he may be conducting an acting workshop with students, rehearsing a play, writing a novel, sculpting, yachting, or taking a call from an Irish guy doing a book about Laurel and Hardy.

I asked him what he was working on, and he told me he had just finished shooting a *Trailer Park Boys* special, *Say Goodnight to the Bad Guys*, which he thought was, 'the best thing we've ever done.'

John is so articulate, energetic, warm, and worldly that you'd be hard pushed to find an easier interviewee. If you have a project, you should give him a shout. You'd probably get a call – if you give him the right area code, that is – and an opening along the lines of, 'Hey, what's on your mind?'

A little under a year later I sent John a draft copy of the book to see if he was happy with everything I had quoted him as having said. He phoned me and said he thought it looked great and pointed out one or two small points of grammar and a few typos. Before he went, I asked him about the TPB film, *Countdown to Liquor Day*, which I knew they were just starting into that autumn. 'Do you know what,' he said enthusiastically, 'I think it's the best thing we've ever done.'

*

Nigel Planer was making dinner when I phoned him which meant we hadn't long to talk. But, having had one postponement already, I was keen to go ahead in case I didn't get another chance. I resolved to keep my questions short but there was a feedback problem, between my Dictaphone and the speaker phone I was using, which meant he could barely hear me so I had to call him back on my mobile. Which then led to another problem, as the speaker on my mobile phone was so poor. It was all very Neil-in-the-Young-Ones, appropriately enough.

We did manage to have a conversation, through, and Nigel suggested several things – among them how kids enjoy laughing at Laurel and Hardy because they are laughing at grown-ups, at a silly version of their parents – that he seemed to think everyone else would have observed but actually no one had. When we had finished, through the crackles and the whirs, I thanked him and asked for an address I could send a small gift on to, and he seemed genuinely surprised and pleased.

A few weeks later, I received an odd black-and-white postcard featuring a photo of a man holding a cabbage. It was one of those quirky postcards you get in gift shops. Written on the back, in green biro, was the following note:

> **Dear Barry, Thank you very much for sending me the DVDs, it's very kind of you. I put them on and great to hear genuine laughter coming from my nine-year-old son. Still works on me too. Best of luck with book! Nigel Planer.**

So maybe, however this book is received, I can point to one small piece of happiness I posted into this world.

*

Although I only interviewed **Graham Linehan** for this book, I also spoke briefly to his *Father Ted* co-writer, **Arthur Mathews**. And having begun to get used to the workings of 'theatrical agents' and 'talent management', it all came about in an endearingly casual way.

Ardal O'Hanlon said several times that the writers of Father Ted were influenced by Laurel and Hardy and at the end of our interview he asked if I wanted him to pass them on an email for me. 'Great,' I said, 'Please do.' Then we parted and I walked back from Ranelagh to where I work at University College Dublin.

Within an hour, I got an email with the header 're Laurel and Hardy' which read:

> **Dear Barry,**
>
> **Hello, there!**
>
> **Ardal told me you were interested in talking to me? I'm sure he was exaggerating.**
>
> **My number is 087 0000000 in case he wasn't.**

best,

Graham

Brilliant, I thought, a third interview and with someone who has done an extremely rare thing in sitcom: written more than one successful one. But before I'd even replied, I got another.

Hello Barry -

Ardal gave me your e-mail.

If you want to ring me this afternoon, I'm on 041 0000000.

- Arthur Mathews

My God, they were queueing up! I finished the email to Graham Linehan and phoned Arthur Mathews. His manner on the phone was just as accessible and easy going as his email had suggested it would be. 'I wasn't a huge Laurel and Hardy fan,' he told me, 'but I did admire them and could see that they were ahead of their time. I liked that slow methodical abuse of it all.'

Arthur Mathews was more into the Marx Brothers, it turned out, and even suggested some films I should watch. So I thanked him for his time and he told me to give him a shout if I had any other questions.

Graham Linehan was equally down to earth and equally easy to talk to. I asked him about this very thing and put it to him that if, as a comedy writer, you're looking at the silliness and baseness of life, these things soak into your skin and keep your feet on the ground.

'I think we all get tricked into taking ourselves too seriously at one time or another,' he reflected. 'That's why it's never a good idea to read reviews because the good ones can make you feel too good about yourself and the bad ones can make you feel too bad. As I said, we're really only sitting at the children's table with sitcom.'

This may be so in the eyes of some people but it's harder (if you look at the hit rate) to write a successful sitcom than it is to write a successful anything else. I put this to him.

'Well, I do think it's harder to write a good sitcom than to write a good play, for example. It's also harder to raise a laugh in a film or a TV show than it is to raise a laugh in the theatre; people will laugh at anything in the theatre.

'In the end, though, I think you've got to have some perspective because you're writing some little half-hour thing that comes on before *Wife Swap*, so you can't go mad thinking you're an artist of whatever. Maybe you've just got me on a day when I'm not taking myself seriously [laughs]. Tomorrow I'll be right back to taking myself seriously.'

I wouldn't imagine so.

*

Richard Wilson stumped me with a question early in our interview. (I thought I was supposed to ask the questions.) He said, 'I always think Stan Laurel is the consummate actor. He can tell you what he is thinking with the raise of an eyebrow; it's extraordinarily subtle. I think Oliver is a bit over the top…I look upon Stan as the real actor, somehow.' There was a pause and then he added, 'Do you agree with that?'

I didn't have much of an answer ready, but it certainly made me think. Then, and long after. In truth, I had always thought that Hardy was more real, Stan more surreal. I never felt that either was better than the other or funnier but it was Hardy that communicated with the audience and bolted everything to the ground.

Richard Wilson's question really made me look at the films differently. I realised how simple many of Stan's actions are. His character spends his time largely trying to keep out of other people's way – unsuccessfully – and it was Richard Wilson that made me see this. He spoke of 'openness' and 'believability' and of 'knowing who you are' and 'letting the audience look in'. It was very revealing.

I think Richard Wilson – as both actor and director – is probably someone who always asks questions. 'I'm acting at the moment,' he told me, 'in a long-running series [*Merlin*] so I'm in front of the camera a great deal, and I'm still trying to work out what acting's all about. It's still a mystery.'

At the end, he asked me yet another question or rather turned one of mine back on itself. 'Laurel and Hardy certainly surpass Chaplin and Buster Keaton,' he said. 'And why do you think that is,' I asked him. 'I don't know,' he replied and then laughed, 'I thought *you* might tell *me*.'

*

Barry Cryer is a comedy connoisseur. His knowledge and insight are unparalleled, and he is so down to earth that it was easy to just keep firing questions at him. Enjoyable too. And he has an amazing list of comedy name-drops: 'Eric [Morecambe] once said to me…'; 'When I was writing for Les Dawson…'; 'Jack Benny…'; 'Joan Rivers…' His work with both British and American stars allowed me to ask him about something that I have always been intrigued by – which was also relevant to Laurel and Hardy – namely, the difference between sitcoms on either side of the Atlantic.

'There's a big divide, I find, in American and British comedy. We tend to love losers; losing's funny, success isn't. Americans, even if you watch something like *Friends*, everybody's doing smart lines. And they're meant to be losers but you think: not really. In Britain, we really do losers [laughs] and we like them because there are more failures in the world than winners so you can identify with them.'

It has often struck me that Laurel and Hardy were more like a British sitcom – fractious, scruffy, base – and that's what made them more popular on this side of the water. Barry Cryer reflected on the same point.

'They probably thought, after their great careers had ended, that they were has-beens. Then they came to Europe on a stage-tour, and I don't think they quite expected the power of the reaction they got…the sheer love. I think they were very moved by that.'

I asked him about the slightly urbane and distanced style – as I would observe it – of American sitcoms. 'Well, I do admire them enormously,' he said, 'but I was listening to an episode of *Friends*, recently, and it was mechanical. It was brilliant but it was line, line, line, laugh. And the laugh didn't sound natural. Audiences don't laugh like that. And I was sure it was canned laughter. Or you would record the audience on the night but tape the bits you want of the laughter. There's something a bit clinical about it. You can always tell the difference between real laughter and manufactured laughter.

'My absolute favourite was *Cheers*, the skill of the writing and the performance…everything. It was a team, ensemble playing; I thought that was superb. And it was full of clearly-defined characters. And like other great sitcoms such as *Dad's Army*, the best lines are not *funny lines*, they're just character lines.'

And then he came out with one more name-drop, someone who was part of the Saturday night schedules for many years of my own childhood. 'I worked with Phil Silvers who said "I love England". I said, "Why?" and he said, "They remember me." His peak was black-and-white television, and he said, "They don't show me, anymore. But I come here and they say, *Oh Bilko's here*, and it's wonderful."'

*

I met **Ray Galton** and **Alan Simpson** at Ray's house in Hampton Court. It was one of only two interviews I did in person (the other was with Ardal O'Hanlon, the rest were over the phone) and the night before it, staying in my brother's flat in Hampstead, I felt a bit odd.

I don't usually get star-struck or giddy on the few occasions I've met my heroes. When I'm doing interviews, I find it's better not to be too gushy but just get on with it. If you start rabbiting on about how much you admire someone, you're really talking about yourself, not them, and it ends up being a poor interview. It represents bad listening, as well, which ironically, is disrespectful.

I felt different about this interview, though. I had grown up with *Steptoe and Son* just as I had Laurel and Hardy. It had been part of my childhood and in particular my teenage years, when, in the late eighties, the BBC screened a run of Steptoe repeats. I knew Harold and Albert Steptoe in the same warm way I knew Stan and Ollie and now I was going to meet the guys who sat down one afternoon and made them up.

It turned out to be a fascinating and enjoyable chat. And, of course, they were utterly down to earth; no star-struck giddiness required. It was particularly interesting when we strayed onto the subject of Hancock – 'Tony' to them – as I had come there with the Steptoes and Laurel and Hardy firmly in my sights but you just can't keep Tony Hancock, the sad clown, out of your eye line. And I was sitting next to the two guys who had written all of his great shows and who knew the man personally.

'What was he like?' I asked unoriginally. I had to.

'Tony was a very intelligent man,' Ray said, 'a very questing man. I think, like a lot of us, he wished he'd stayed at school longer or gone to university. He was very interested in politics and very interested in the ascent of man…where we're all going…what are we doing here. And the role of religion; he wasn't a religious man, himself, but he thought about it. And philosophy…things like that. Art.'

'Did you get on with him?'

'Yeah, we got on alright,' said Alan, 'because we all came up together. Tony was a star before we joined the business, or a rising star, he wasn't quite top of the bill. But we were unknowns, we'd just started. We met him very early on and we actually wrote everything he did, in every medium, for nine years.'

Whether it was through *Steptoe and Son* or before with Hancock, it's hard not to conclude, as many people have, that Ray Galton and Alan Simpson invented the sitcom as we know it today. The key was to have actors – or comedians who acted – not playing to the audience for laughs but playing their part in a situation that was funny. The word they used repeatedly was 'authenticity' and Ray and Alan themselves were authentic. There was no aloofness, no bluster, no third-person references; they were just two guys from London who met and wrote comedy for a living.

'Anyone who goes on flights of self-aggrandisement is an idiot,' said Alan. 'You get prats wanting to be called Sir-whatever. If you have any intelligence at all, the ludicrousness of standing on a plinth because you've done a few films… I could never imagine Stan Laurel, for instance, if he became a straight director, changing his name to Stanley Laurel. But Chaplin became Charles Chaplin and to me that's phoney.'

There was nothing phoney about Alan Simpson or Ray Galton. Easiest interview ever; I don't know why I was so nervous.

*

As a kid, I distinctly remember my mother pointing at **Andrew Sachs** during a TV interview and saying, 'That's Manuel from Fawlty Towers.' I couldn't believe the transformation. How could this mild mannered, polite, friendly gentleman turn himself into one of the most iconic knockabout clowns of television?

'I never find comedy difficult,' he told me. 'A lot of actors say, "Oh comedy is the most difficult," but I find it the easiest. Playing *King Lear* would be much more difficult for me or *Hamlet*, so it's the way one is built. It just appeals to me and I'm at ease with comedy. If there's a comedy element to a character, I love that.'

'What things make you laugh?' I asked.

'Well, it's not difficult to make me laugh but I tend to see, not the humorous side, but the absurd side of life. I think life is an absurd situation; there are the most ridiculous things going on even in the most serious and tragic situations. People go to war when really it shouldn't be necessary. So not funny, exactly, but you think, God, what are we doing on this earth? The way we behave towards each other, and it's horrifying in a way but it's also absurd.'

There's something in this that only struck me after finishing the book. It's something, maybe, that ties all the Laurels and Hardys together, the line of Fawltys and Manuels that runs right through British sitcom. It was prompted by something Eric Sykes – who I was supposed to interview but unfortunately never managed to tie down – said about stupid people. He said that stupid people don't scare him, serious ones do. The people who take themselves seriously, the ones who believe their own guff, they're the ones who do all the damage.

And I thought about Brent and Mainwaring and Fawlty and Ted and Hardy, among many others. If you were a comedy writer or performer, if you had a sense of the absurd and the comical, who would your enemy be? Who would be the butt of your joke? Who would you have in your cross-hairs if it wasn't the very idiot who couldn't see the funny side? The fool who took himself that bit too seriously?

As Andrew explained, 'Really when you analyse it, *Fawlty Towers* is not funny at all. It's a tragedy, isn't it, a tragedy of bad relationships and incompetence and all the things that can go wrong in life. But it's pointed to such a degree that we see the absurd side of that tragedy and laugh at it.'

So speaks Manuel. Not as stupid as he looks.

Other Books from Bennion Kearny

Wolfram Wars: Exposing The Secret Battle in Portugal by Rod Ashley

Wolfram – also known as Tungsten – is about more than electric light bulbs. Its more deadly claim-to-fame rests in its armour-piercing qualities.

During WWII, Wolfram was in great demand with both the Allies and Axis powers who scoured the globe for the precious material; indeed, they deployed huge resources to secure supplies whilst simultaneously doing their best to sabotage and undermine one another.

The greatest beneficiary from these shadowy dealings was Portugal, a neutral country, under the control of the mercurial António de Oliveira Salazar. The sudden surge in demand created great wealth and bustling 'gold rush towns' deep in Portugal's remote mountainous interior, but threatened to undermine Salazar's grand vision for his country.

Wolfram Wars examines the role of Portugal in the Wolfram trade, alongside the exploits of its British, American and German customers. It takes in the glitz and glamour of wartime Lisbon, the mischievous dealings of intelligence services, and includes some of WWII's most interesting spies – spies with code names such as Garbo, Tricycle, and Treasure. A certain young intelligence officer and creator of James Bond – Ian Fleming – also has a role to play.

Other Books from Bennion Kearny

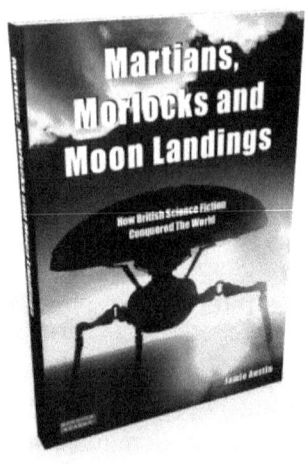

Martians, Morlocks and Moon Landings: How British Science Fiction Conquered The World by Jamie Austin

Science Fiction has long been a part of popular culture. From the colour co-ordinated adventures of Captain Kirk and crew to the city chomping of Godzilla, it is very much a worldwide phenomenon. And it all started over a century ago – in Britain.

From Victorian literature through to the modern day - Martians, Morlocks and Moon Landings explores the genre's development through the imaginations of H G Wells, John Wyndham, George Orwell, Nigel Kneale, and many more. It chronicles the creative minds that foresaw lasers, moon landings, and aggressive walking plants. It charts the socio-political climates which gave rise to Orwell's totalitarian vision, the self-sufficient Survivors, and the cash-strapped Blake's 7. British Science Fiction is a window into contemporary history, laying bare a nation's psyche - occasionally by dressing it up in a foam rubber costume and having it pursue actors down a BBC corridor.

Martians, Morlocks and Moon Landings details the influence of British Science Fiction on the world stage and is a must-read resource for anyone with an interest in the genre.

Other Books from Bennion Kearny

The Doors Examined by Jim Cherry

Jim Morrison, Ray Manzarek, Robby Krieger and John Densmore. Welcome to the known, the unknown, and the in between. *Welcome to The Doors Examined.*

The Doors remain one of the most influential and exciting bands in rock 'n' roll history, and The Doors Examined offers a unique, expressive insight into the history of the band, their influence on culture, and the group's journey following the death of Jim Morrison in Paris in 1971. It starts at the beginning, on a Venice Beach rooftop, and takes the reader on an invigorating journey, from The Whisky a Go-Go to the Dinner Key Auditorium, The Ed Sullivan Show to Père Lachaise Cemetery.

Comprised of selected acclaimed articles from The Doors Examiner, The Doors Examined also serves up original content that assesses seminal albums, how the group's music has influenced other artists, and key people in the band's history; people like Jac Holzman, Paul Rothchild, Bruce Botnick, and Pam Courson.

The Doors Examined is a must read investigation into one of the greatest rock 'n' roll bands of all time.

Other Books from Bennion Kearny

The Hidden Motor: The Psychology of Cycling by Martijn Veltkamp

Cycling is one of the world's great sports. From The Tour de France to the Paris-Roubaix to velodromes across the globe, it encompasses many disciplines: from climbing mountains to massed sprints to the loneliness of the time trial.

But what separates race winners from the nearly men? Top cyclists are physically similar, train the right way, eat the right things, and yet there is something that separates them. It's their hidden engine – not a secret mechanical aid - but what's between their ears that makes the difference.

In this superbly-researched and accessible book for fans of cycling, psychologist and cycling author Martijn Veltkamp gets to the heart of the supremely demanding and challenging sport of professional cycling, and the mental side of performance that drives success. He addresses fundamental questions in an easy-to-read way, including: what motivates riders and how does motivation affect performance? Where does a rider's fear of descending originate from, and how do you get rid of it? Why do some cyclists succumb under pressure, whilst others do not? Why is cycling on your own mentally more challenging than when in a group?

www.ingramcontent.com/pod-product-compliance
Lightning Source LLC
LaVergne TN
LVHW051559080426
835510LV00020B/3056